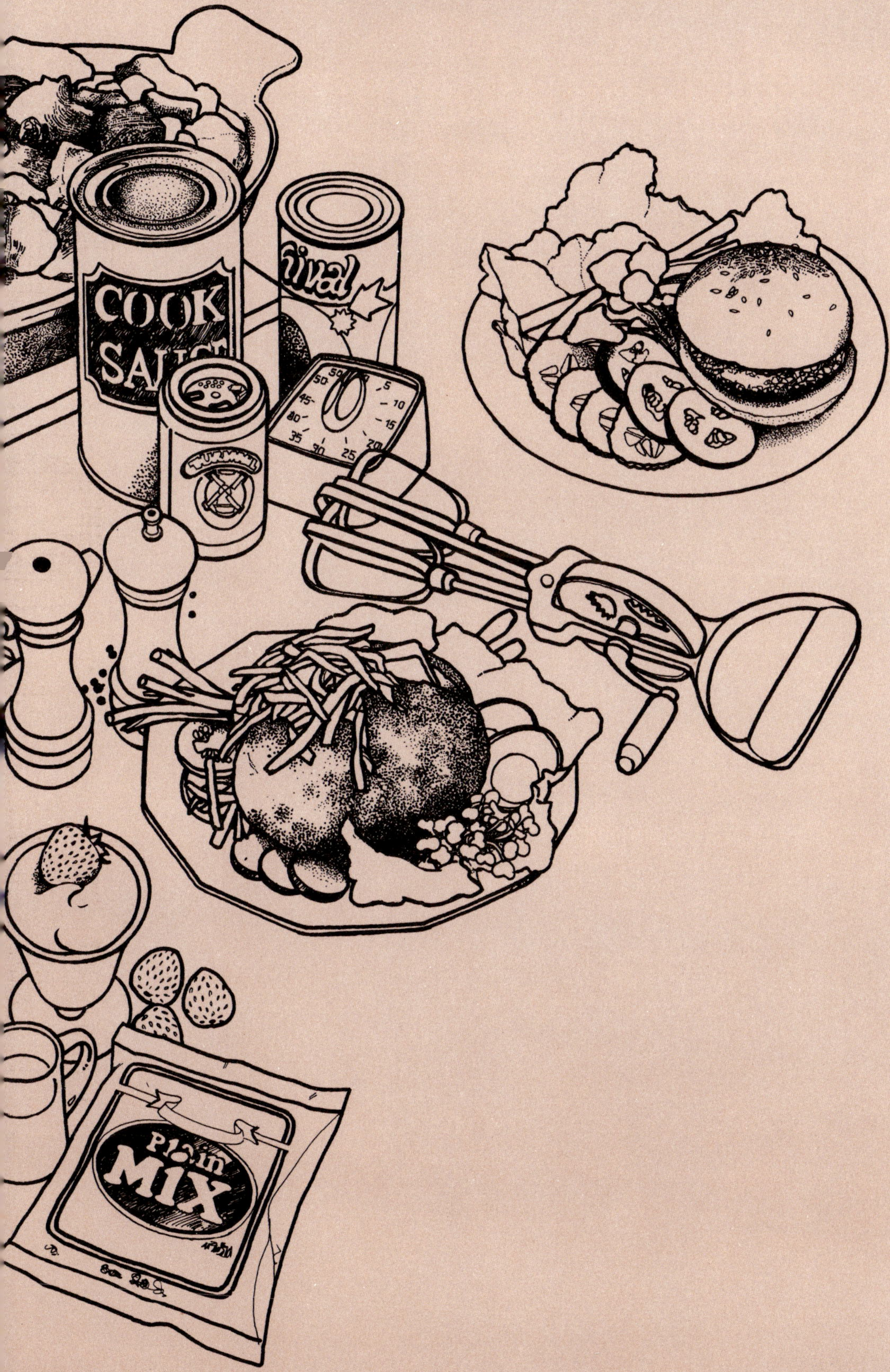
COOK
Plain
MIX

FAST FOOD

Edited by
Alison Kerr

octopus

Contents

Introduction 7
For Brunch or Lunch 8
What's in the Cupboard? 26
Sandwiches Hot and Cold 32
Speedy Salads 42
Simple Suppers 48
Short and Sweet 63
Index 76

NOTES

All measurements in this book are given in Metric, Imperial and American. Follow one set only because they are not interchangeable.

Standard spoon measurements are used in all recipes
1 tablespoon = one 15 ml spoon
1 teaspoon = one 5 ml spoon
All spoon measurements are level.

Use freshly ground black pepper where pepper is specified.

Ovens and grills (broilers) should be preheated to the specified temperature or heat setting.

**This edition first published 1981 by
Octopus Books Limited
59 Grosvenor Street, London W1**

© 1981 Octopus Books Limited

ISBN 0 7064 1510 8

Produced and printed in Hong Kong by
Mandarin Publishers Limited
22a Westlands Road, Quarry Bay, Hong Kong

Cover photography by Paul Williams

Frontispiece: DANISH OPEN SANDWICHES *(page 40)*
(Photograph: The Danish Centre)

INTRODUCTION

After a high-speed, jam-packed, frantic day at work, how many times have you heard people say, on the bus or in the subway: 'I never have time to cook', or 'I can't be bothered to cook', or 'I can't even boil an egg'.

In the last few years, more and more chicken, taco, kebab and curry takeaways have sprung up to compete with the old faithful hamburger, Chinese and fish and chips, and it's no mystery why. More wives work now than ever before, more young people are leaving home and setting up on their own, and people are working harder and playing harder.

For those who lead busy lives, cooking may come low on the list of priorities, but this book will show how cheap, delicious and even impressive nosh can be produced without breaking the bank, your nails or your date!

The art and sheer fun of cooking can be made to fit in with a hectic pace. Instead of a meal out on a summer night, why not invite friends round for a salad at your place – they can bring the wine! How about toasted sandwiches with hot soup after a battle at the Christmas sales or crêpes with delicious fillings to impress your mother-in-law?

You won't need a shopping list longer than your arm, or a lot of fancy equipment. Just take a look in the refrigerator, because simple ingredients can make super meals, with luscious desserts too. Even a boring old sandwich can have a touch of class with unusual fillings and garnishes. Don't just boil the egg or grill the cheese – turn a snack into a feast.

If you've never tried much cooking before, welcome to a new experience. If you thought cooking was a thing of the past, welcome back!

FOR BRUNCH OR LUNCH

Cheesy Beef Pizzas

METRIC/IMPERIAL
1 quantity basic scone pizza dough (see page 11)
15 g/½ oz butter or margarine
1 large onion, sliced
1 garlic clove, crushed
500 g/1 lb minced beef
pinch of dried mixed herbs
salt and pepper
50 g/2 oz Cheddar cheese, grated
4 tomato slices to garnish

AMERICAN
1 quantity basic biscuit pizza dough (see page 11)
1 tablespoon butter or margarine
1 large onion, sliced
1 garlic clove, crushed
1 lb ground beef
pinch of dried mixed herbs
salt and pepper
½ cup grated Cheddar cheese
4 tomato slices to garnish

Roll out the dough to one large or four smaller rounds about 1 cm/½ inch thick and transfer to a greased baking sheet. Push up the edge of the rounds to make a rim.

Melt the butter or margarine in a frying pan (skillet), add the onion and garlic and fry until softened. Add the beef and brown well. Drain off all excess fat, then stir in the herbs and salt and pepper to taste.

Spread the beef mixture over the dough rounds and sprinkle with the cheese. Bake in a preheated moderately hot oven (200°C/400°F, Gas Mark 6) for 20 to 25 minutes for a large pizza and 15 to 20 minutes for small pizzas. Garnish with the tomato slices.
Serves 2 to 4

Quick variation:
Use 1 × 425 g/15 oz can of minced (ground) beef.

CHEESY BEEF PIZZAS
(Photograph: Canned Food Advisory Service)

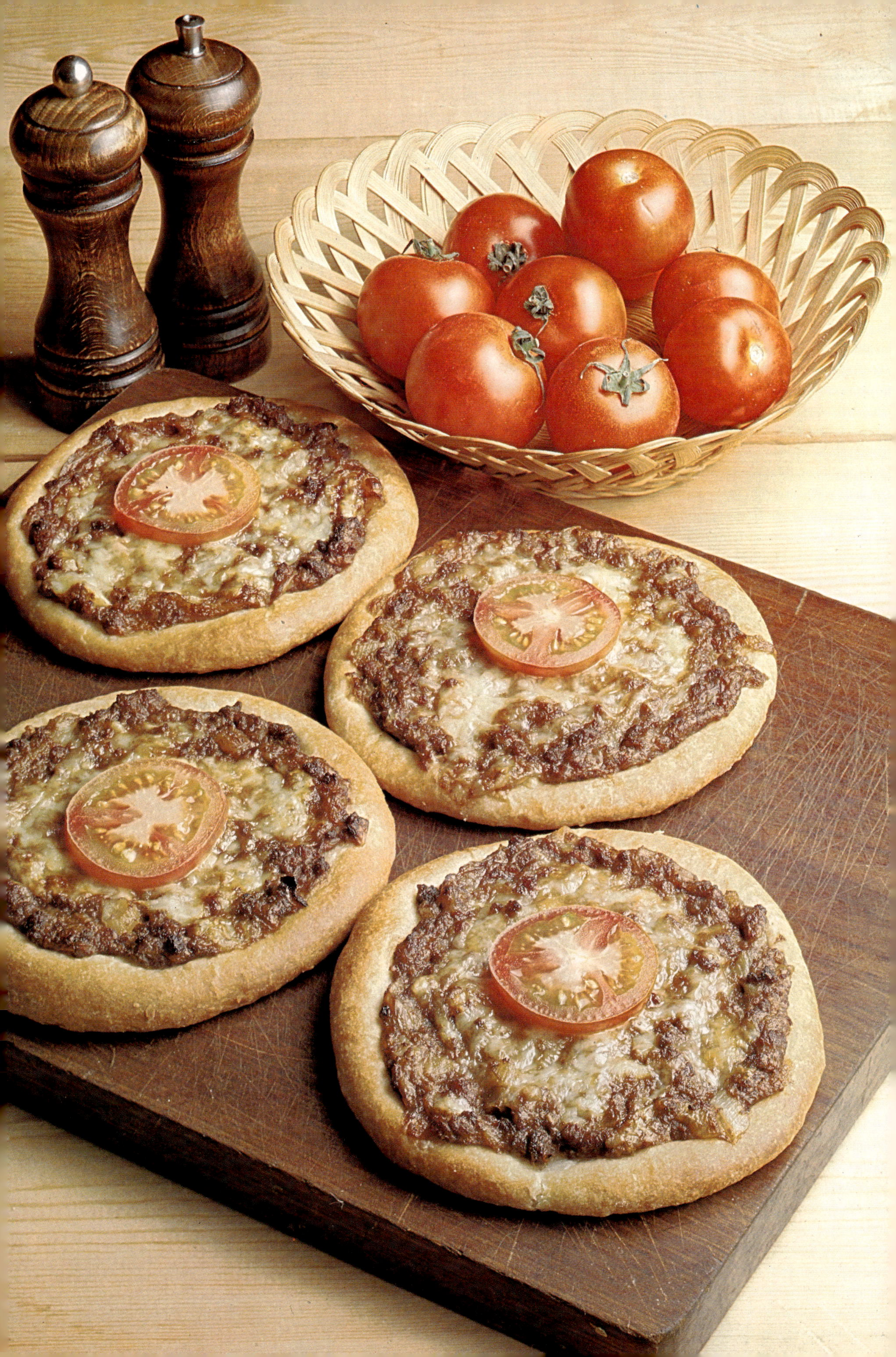

Stuffed Baked Potatoes

METRIC/IMPERIAL
4 potatoes
1 packet white sauce mix
milk
100 g/4 oz cooked ham, chopped
1 tablespoon chopped chives
1 tablespoon chopped parsley
1 tablespoon French mustard
100 g/4 oz cheese, grated

AMERICAN
4 potatoes
1 package white sauce mix
milk
½ cup chopped cooked ham
1 tablespoon chopped chives
1 tablespoon chopped parsley
1 tablespoon French mustard
1 cup grated cheese

Bake the potatoes in a preheated moderate oven (180°C/350°F, Gas Mark 4) for 1 to 1½ hours or until tender. Cut the potatoes in half and scoop out the flesh. Make up the sauce with milk, according to the directions on the packet. Mix with the potato flesh, then add the ham, herbs and mustard. Replace in the potato skins. Place in a flameproof dish. Sprinkle with the cheese and grill (broil) until it is melted and golden.

Bacon and Mushroom
Fry 2 bacon rashers (slices), chopped, and 50 g /2 oz (½ cup) sliced mushrooms, in 40 g/1½ oz (3 tablespoons) butter. Mix with the scooped-out potato flesh and season to taste with salt and pepper. Garnish with parsley.

Celery and Sausage
Mix the scooped-out potato flesh with ½ × 300 g/11½ oz can condensed celery soup, 100 g/4 oz (½ cup) chopped German salami or garlic sausage, most of 100 g/4 oz (1 cup) grated Gouda cheese, and salt and pepper to taste. Fill the potato skins, sprinkle with the remaining cheese and grill (broil) as above.

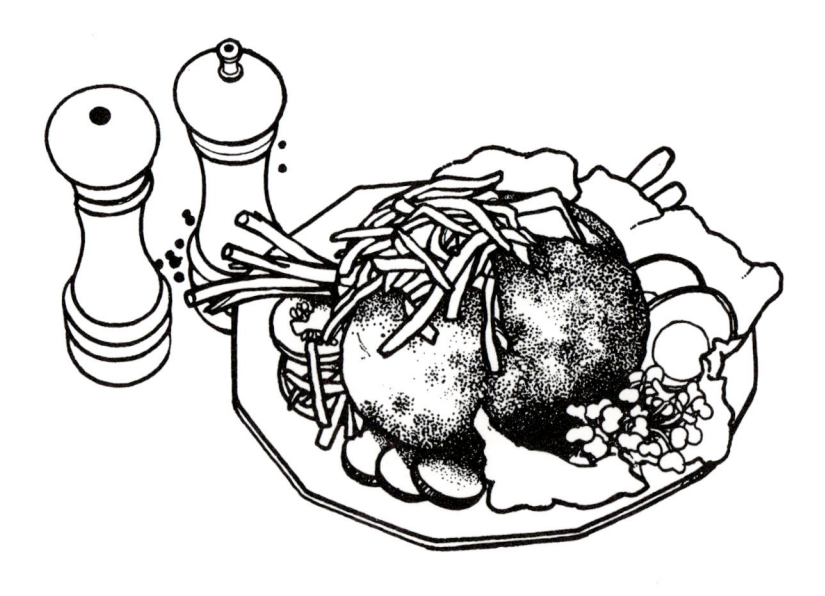

Scone (Biscuit) Pizza

METRIC/IMPERIAL
225 g/8 oz self-raising flour
½ teaspoon salt
50 g/2 oz butter
150 ml/¼ pint milk
Topping:
15 g/½ oz butter
1 onion, sliced
3 tomatoes, thinly sliced
salt and pepper
½ teaspoon dried mixed herbs
175 g/6 oz Cheddar cheese, grated
2 streaky bacon rashers, rinded and cut into strips
black olives

AMERICAN
2 cups self-rising flour
½ teaspoon salt
4 tablespoons butter
⅔ cup milk
Topping:
1 tablespoon butter
1 onion, sliced
3 tomatoes, thinly sliced
salt and pepper
½ teaspoon dried mixed herbs
1½ cups grated Cheddar cheese
2 bacon slices, cut into strips
ripe olives

Sift the flour and salt into a bowl. Rub in the butter. Add the milk and mix to a soft dough. Turn onto a floured board and knead until smooth. Roll out to one large or four small circles about 1 cm/½ inch thick. Place on a greased baking sheet.

For the topping, melt the butter in a frying pan (skillet), add the onion and fry until softened. Place on the pizza. Top with the tomatoes, salt and pepper, herbs and cheese. Make a lattice with the bacon strips. Place the olives in the lattice windows. Bake in a preheated hot oven (220°C/425°F, Gas Mark 7) for 15 to 20 minutes.

Variations:
Use 1 × 225 g/8 oz can tomatoes, drained, instead of fresh tomatoes.

Make a lattice with canned sardines, kipper fillets, anchovies or various cooked sausages.

Use other cheeses.

Aubergine (Eggplant) Rarebit

METRIC/IMPERIAL	AMERICAN
2 aubergines, sliced	2 eggplants, sliced
salt	salt
oil	oil
100 g/4 oz mild Cheddar cheese, grated	1 cup grated mild Cheddar cheese
parsley sprigs to garnish	parsley sprigs to garnish

Salt the aubergine (eggplant) slices and leave to drain for 30 minutes. Rinse and pat dry with paper towels. Brush lightly with oil and grill (broil) for 10 minutes on each side. Place on a flameproof dish and cover with the grated cheese. Grill (broil) until lightly browned. Serve at once, garnished with parsley.

Cottage Toasties

METRIC/IMPERIAL	AMERICAN
4 tomatoes, sliced	4 tomatoes, sliced
100 g/4 oz button mushrooms, sliced	1 cup sliced button mushrooms
4 slices of bread, toasted	4 slices of bread, toasted
25 g/1 oz dried milk	$\frac{1}{3}$ cup dried milk
225 g/8 oz cottage cheese with sweetcorn and peppers	1 cup cottage cheese with corn kernels and peppers
4 spring onions, chopped	4 scallions, chopped
salt and pepper	salt and pepper

Arrange the tomatoes and mushrooms on the toast. Mix together the dried milk, cottage cheese, spring onions (scallions) and salt and pepper to taste. Pile on the toast and grill (broil) until golden brown. Serve with salad.

AUBERGINE (EGGPLANT) RAREBIT
(Photograph: Carmel Produce Information Bureau)

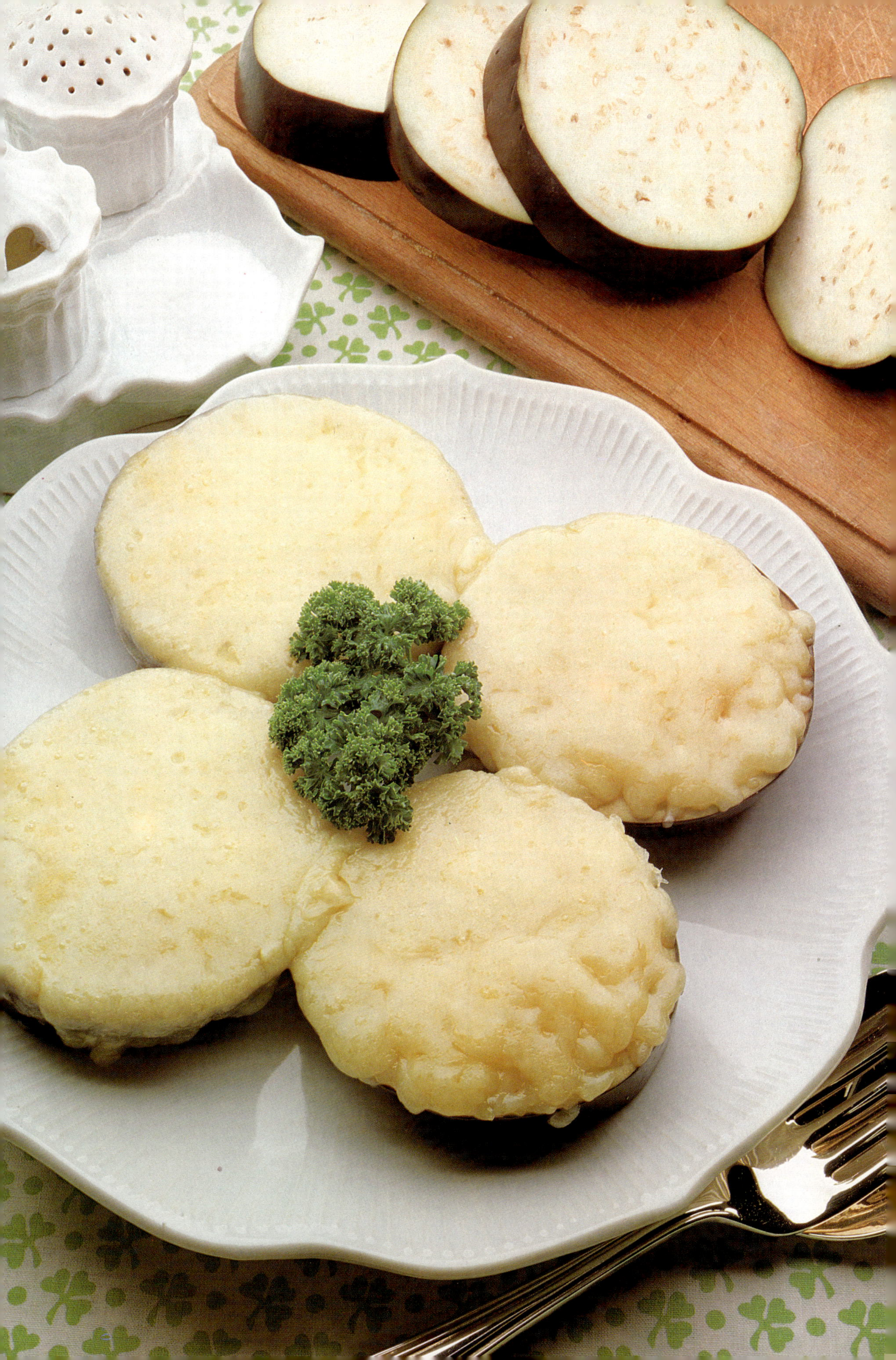

Eggs Florentine

METRIC/IMPERIAL
25 g/1 oz butter
500 g/1 lb tomatoes, skinned and quartered
500 g/1 lb spinach, cooked and chopped
pinch of grated nutmeg
salt and pepper
8 hot soft-boiled eggs
Sauce:
15 g/½ oz butter
15 g/½ oz flour
300 ml/½ pint milk
50 g/2 oz cheese, grated
1 tablespoon grated Parmesan cheese

AMERICAN
2 tablespoons butter
1 lb tomatoes, skinned and quartered
1 lb spinach, cooked and chopped
pinch of grated nutmeg
salt and pepper
8 hot soft-cooked eggs
Sauce:
1 tablespoon butter
2 tablespoons flour
1¼ cups milk
½ cup grated cheese
1 tablespoon grated Parmesan cheese

Melt 15 g/½ oz (1 tablespoon) of the butter in a frying pan (skillet), add the tomatoes and fry for 3 to 4 minutes. Transfer to a baking dish. Melt the rest of the butter, add the spinach and toss with the nutmeg and salt and pepper to taste. Place the spinach on the tomatoes and top with the eggs. Keep hot.

To make the sauce, melt the butter in a saucepan, stir in the flour and cook for 1 minute. Gradually stir in the milk and bring to the boil. Simmer until thickened, then stir in the grated cheese. Pour the sauce over the eggs. Sprinkle the Parmesan on top and grill (broil) for 3 to 4 minutes.

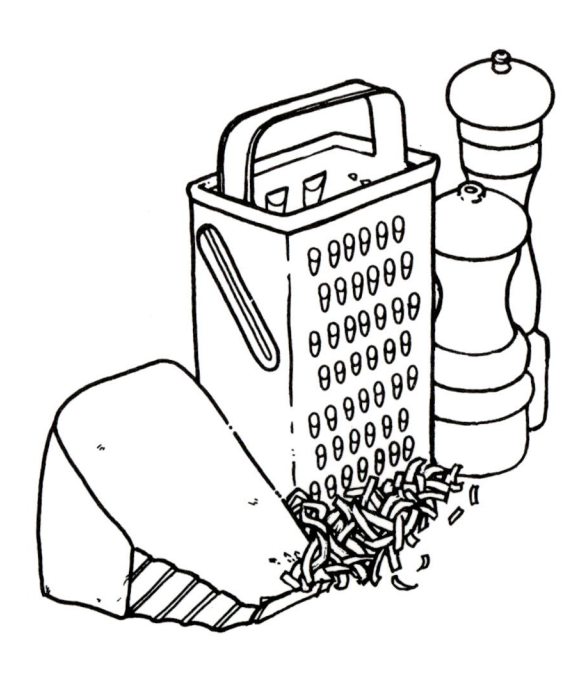

Scrambled Eggs Supreme

METRIC/IMPERIAL
500 g/1 lb hot mashed potatoes
5 eggs
salt and pepper
25 g/1 oz lard
225 g/8 oz skinless sausages, cut into 1 cm/½ inch pieces
1 green pepper, cored, seeded and sliced
1 onion, chopped
1 × 275 g/10 oz can cream-style sweetcorn
25 g/1 oz cheese, grated

AMERICAN
2 cups hot mashed potatoes
5 eggs
salt and pepper
2 tablespoons shortening
½ lb skinless sausages, cut into ½ inch pieces
1 green pepper, cored, seeded and sliced
1 onion, chopped
1 × 10 oz can cream-style corn kernels
¼ cup grated cheese

Mix together the potato, one of the eggs and salt and pepper to taste. Use this to cover the bottom and sides of a greased flameproof serving dish. Keep hot.

Melt the lard (shortening) in a frying pan (skillet), add the sausages, green pepper and onion and fry until the sausage pieces are lightly browned. Stir in the corn. Beat together the remaining eggs and salt and pepper to taste. Add to the pan and cook gently until the eggs are lightly scrambled. Tip into the potato-lined dish and sprinkle with the cheese. Grill (broil) until the top is golden brown and bubbling.

Egg Hubble Bubble

METRIC/IMPERIAL
50 g/2 oz butter
175 g/6 oz potatoes, cooked and chopped
4 tomatoes, skinned and quartered
100 g/4 oz mushrooms, quartered
175 g/6 oz cooked broad beans or peas
salt and pepper
6 eggs, beaten
50 g/2 oz Cheddar cheese, grated

AMERICAN
4 tablespoons butter
1 cup chopped cooked potatoes
4 tomatoes, skinned and quartered
1 cup quartered mushrooms
1 cup cooked lima beans or peas
salt and pepper
6 eggs, beaten
½ cup grated Cheddar cheese

Melt the butter in a frying pan (skillet), add the potatoes and fry until well browned. Stir in the tomatoes and mushrooms and fry lightly. Add the beans or peas and salt and pepper to taste. Heat gently. Pour the eggs over the vegetables and sprinkle the cheese on top. Cover and leave to cook gently until just set.

Corn Scramble

METRIC/IMPERIAL
25 g/1 oz margarine
2 tablespoons milk
1 × 200 g/7 oz can sweet corn,
  drained
4 eggs, beaten
salt and pepper
4 crusty rolls

AMERICAN
1 oz margarine
2 tablespoons milk
1 × 7 oz can corn kernels,
  drained
4 eggs, beaten
salt and pepper
4 crusty rolls

Heat the margarine and milk in a saucepan. Add the corn. Season the beaten eggs with salt and pepper, then add to the corn and scramble lightly. Serve with the rolls.

Pitta Kebab

METRIC/IMPERIAL
1 kg/2 lb boned leg of lamb, cut into
  2.5 cm/1 inch cubes
4 tablespoons oil
juice of 2 lemons
2 fresh thyme sprigs, or 1 teaspoon
  dried thyme
salt and pepper
4 pitta breads, split open
To serve:
cucumber slices
tomato slices
onion rings
lettuce leaves, shredded
black olives

AMERICAN
2 lb boned leg of lamb, cut into
  1 inch cubes
$\frac{1}{4}$ cup oil
juice of 2 lemons
2 fresh thyme sprigs, or 1 teaspoon
  dried thyme
salt and pepper
4 pitta breads, split open
To serve:
cucumber slices
tomato slices
onion rings
lettuce leaves, shredded
ripe olives

Put the lamb cubes into a bowl and sprinkle over the oil and lemon juice. Add the thyme and salt and pepper to taste. Turn the lamb cubes to coat well. Leave to marinate for at least 30 minutes, or longer if possible.

Thread the lamb cubes onto 4 skewers, reserving the marinade. Grill (broil), or cook over hot coals on a barbecue, until the meat is cooked through to your taste. Turn and baste with the reserved marinade from time to time.

Meanwhile, heat the pitta in a preheated moderately hot oven (200°C/400°F, Gas Mark 6) for about 10 minutes.

Slide the lamb cubes off the skewers and stuff into the pocket in the pitta. Add cucumber and tomato slices, onion rings, lettuce leaves and black (ripe) olives and serve.

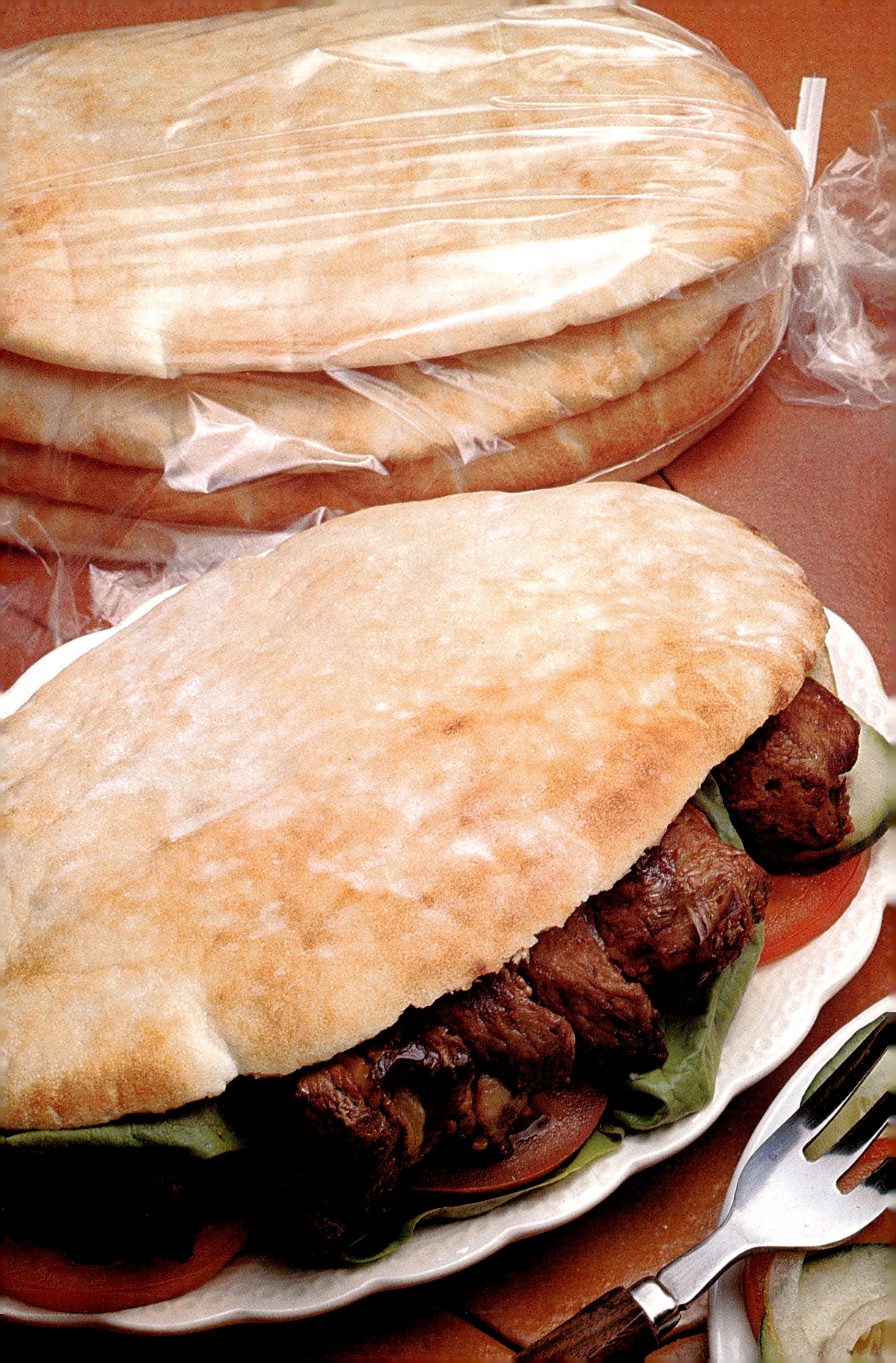

Thirty-Minute Pan Fry

METRIC/IMPERIAL
2 tablespoons oil
1 onion, sliced
1 green pepper, cored, seeded and sliced
500 g/1 lb lamb's liver, cut into 1 cm/½ inch strips
25 g/1 oz flour
1 × 400 g/14 oz can tomatoes
1 tablespoon Worcestershire sauce
½ teaspoon dried oregano
75 g/3 oz pasta shells
salt and pepper

AMERICAN
2 tablespoons oil
1 onion, sliced
1 green pepper, cored, seeded and sliced
1 lb lamb liver, cut into ½ inch strips
¼ cup flour
1 × 14 oz can tomatoes
1 tablespoon Worcestershire sauce
½ teaspoon dried oregano
⅔ cup pasta shells
salt and pepper

Heat the oil in a large frying pan (skillet), add the onion and fry until softened. Add the green pepper and fry for about 2 minutes. Coat the liver strips with the flour. Add to the vegetables and fry, stirring, until brown on all sides. Stir in the tomatoes, Worcestershire sauce and herbs. Cover and cook for 10 minutes.

Meanwhile, cook the pasta in boiling water until tender. Drain well and add to the pan. Season to taste with salt and pepper and cook for a further 5 minutes. Serve with a green vegetable or salad.

German Breakfast Platter

METRIC/IMPERIAL
15 g/½ oz butter
2 streaky bacon rashers
8 cocktail sausages
4 tomatoes
4 eggs
60 ml/2 fl oz milk
salt and pepper
chopped chives, to garnish
hot buttered toast

AMERICAN
1 tablespoon butter
2 bacon slices
8 link sausages
4 tomatoes
4 eggs
¼ cup milk
salt and pepper
chopped chives, to garnish
hot buttered toast

Melt and brown the butter in a large frying pan (skillet). Add the bacon and sausages and fry until well cooked. Remove and keep warm. Cut the tomatoes in half and cook cut side down. Beat the eggs, milk, salt and pepper together and pour over the tomatoes. Cook until set. Replace the bacon and sausages and garnish with the chives. Serve with hot buttered toast.

Kedgeree

METRIC/IMPERIAL
175 g/6 oz smoked haddock
50 g/2 oz butter
175 g/6 oz cooked rice
3 hard-boiled eggs, chopped
salt and pepper
1 egg, beaten
Garnish:
1 hard-boiled egg, sliced
chopped parsley

AMERICAN
1 cup smoked haddock
¼ cup butter
1 cup cooked rice
3 hard-cooked eggs, chopped
salt and pepper
1 egg, beaten
Garnish:
1 hard-cooked egg, sliced
chopped parsley

Simmer the fish in salted water for about 10 minutes, drain and flake. Melt the butter and stir in the rice and fish. Mix in the eggs and salt and pepper to taste. Stir in the beaten egg and when the mixture is creamy, serve hot, garnished with the sliced egg and chopped parsley.

Bratwurst Kedgeree

METRIC/IMPERIAL
6 bratwurst sausages
50 g/2 oz butter
4 tablespoons oil
2 onions, sliced
2 sticks celery, sliced
¼ teaspoon curry powder
¼ teaspoon turmeric
225 g/8 oz cooked long grain rice
20 Chinese leaves
parsley sprig to garnish

AMERICAN
6 bratwurst sausages
4 tablespoons butter
¼ cup oil
2 onions, sliced
2 stalks celery, sliced
¼ teaspoon curry powder
¼ teaspoon turmeric
1½ cups cooked long grain rice
20 Chinese leaves (bok choy)
parsley sprig to garnish

Grill (broil) the sausages for 8 to 10 minutes on each side or until well cooked.

Meanwhile, melt the butter with the oil in a frying pan (skillet), add the onions and celery and fry until softened. Stir in the curry powder and turmeric. Add the rice and toss well. Heat through gently.

Line a salad bowl with the Chinese leaves and pile the rice mixture in the centre. Cut the sausages into 1 cm/½ inch diagonal slices and overlap to form a border inside the leaves. Garnish with parsley and serve hot.

Noodles Romanoff

METRIC/IMPERIAL
1 × 200 g/7 oz packet barbecue
 flavoured noodles
2 cloves garlic, crushed
300 ml/½ pint soured cream
4 tablespoons grated Parmesan cheese
1 tablespoon chives, chopped
½ green pepper, cored, seeded and
 chopped
salt and pepper
Garnish:
grated Parmesan cheese
10 salami rolls

AMERICAN
1 × 7 oz package barbecue
 flavoured noodles
2 cloves garlic, crushed
1¼ cups soured cream
4 tablespoons grated Parmesan cheese
1 tablespoon chopped chives
½ green pepper, cored, seeded and
 chopped
salt and pepper
Garnish:
grated Parmesan cheese
10 salami rolls

Make up the noodles according to the package. Stir in the other ingredients and cook gently for 1 minute. Serve garnished with Parmesan and rolls of salami.

Chinese Noodles

METRIC/IMPERIAL
225 g/8 oz vermicelli noodles
boiling chicken stock
4 tablespoons oil
6 spring onions, chopped
50 g/2 oz flaked almonds
225 g/8 oz cooked chicken meat,
 diced
2 carrots, grated
50 g/2 oz button mushrooms, sliced
salt and pepper
soy sauce

AMERICAN
½ lb vermicelli noodles
boiling chicken stock
¼ cup oil
6 scallions, chopped
½ cup flaked almonds
1 cup finely chopped cooked chicken
 meat
2 carrots, grated
½ cup sliced button mushrooms
salt and pepper
soy sauce

Cook the noodles in boiling chicken stock until they are just tender. Meanwhile, heat the oil in a frying pan (skillet), add the spring onions (scallions), almonds, chicken, carrots and mushrooms and stir-fry for about 4 minutes.

Drain the noodles well, then stir into the chicken mixture with salt, pepper and soy sauce to taste. Cook for a further 4 minutes, stirring well.

CHINESE NOODLES
(Photograph: Kellogg Company)

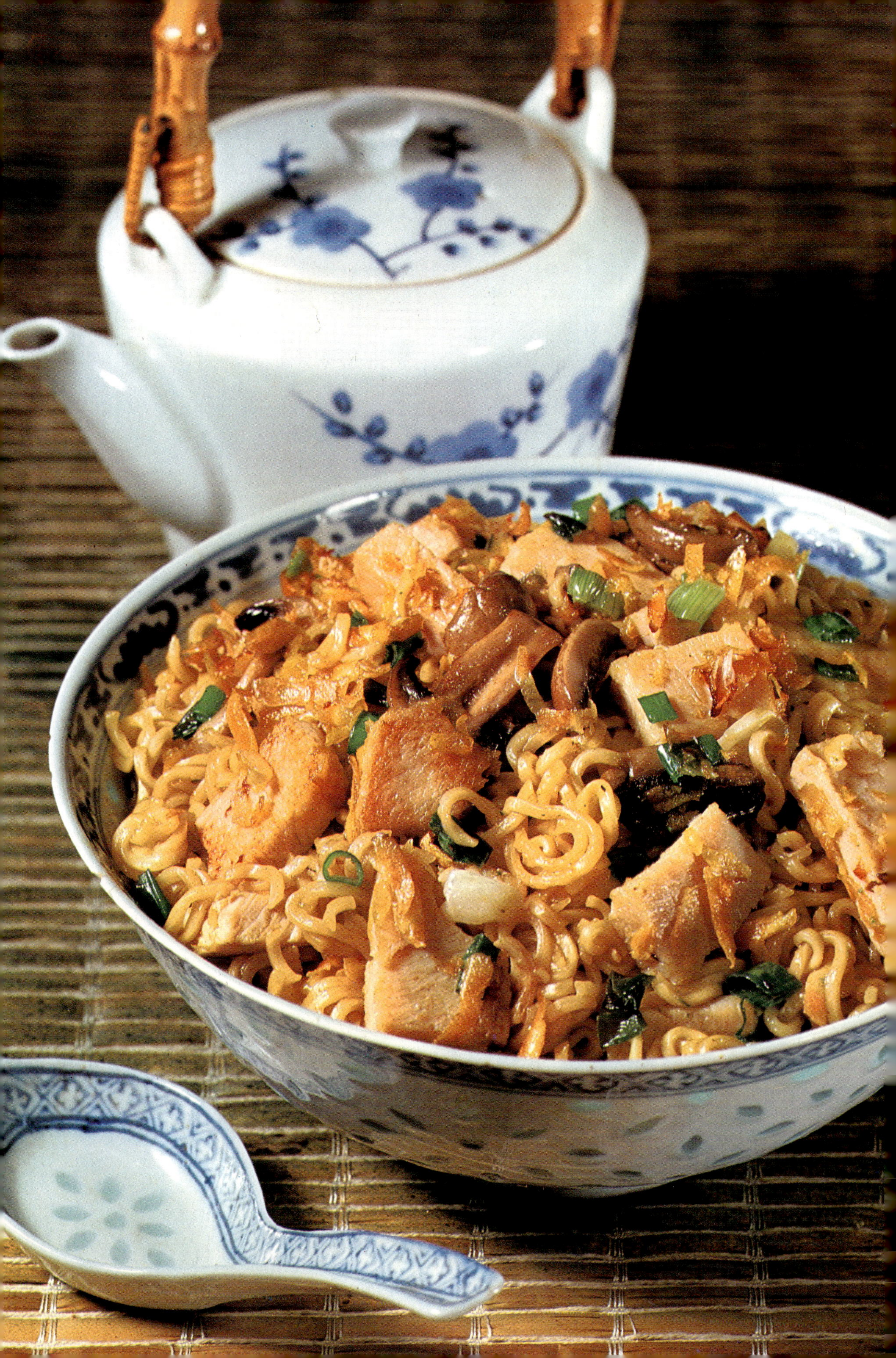

Savoury Crêpes

METRIC/IMPERIAL
100 g/4 oz plain flour
pinch of salt
1 egg
300 ml/½ pint milk
oil for cooking

AMERICAN
1 cup all-purpose flour
pinch of salt
1 egg
1¼ cups milk
oil for cooking

Sift the flour and salt into a bowl. Make a well in the centre and add the egg. Add the milk gradually, beating all the time.

Warm an 18 cm/7 inch frying pan (skillet) over moderate heat, then wipe with an oiled paper towel. Pour in sufficient batter to just cover the base, tilting the pan to spread evenly. Cook gently, until the underside of the crêpe is golden. Toss or turn, using a spatula or palette knife and cook the other side. Slide onto a warmed plate and keep hot. Repeat with the remaining batter.

This recipe makes 8 crêpes. They can be made in advance and kept in the refrigerator or freezer.

Savoury filled crêpes can be served plain, or covered with a sauce or grated cheese, then lightly browned under the grill (broiler) or in a hot oven. A can of condensed soup or cook-in sauce may be used as a fast alternative to a sauce. Here are some suggested fillings:

Leek and Bacon Crêpes
Fry 225 g/8 oz (1 cup) thinly sliced leeks and 3 to 4 bacon rashers (slices), diced, in 40 g/1½ oz (3 tablespoons) butter. Drain well and mix with ½ teaspoon prepared mustard and salt and pepper to taste.

Tomato Crêpes
Fry 1 onion, chopped, and 3 to 4 bacon rashers (slices), chopped, in 25 g/1 oz (2 tablespoons) butter. Stir in 1 × 400 g/14 oz can tomatoes and simmer until thick. Season to taste with salt and pepper.

Chicken Crêpes
Mix 350 g/12 oz (1½ cups) minced (ground) cooked chicken meat with a pinch of grated nutmeg. Add Worcestershire sauce and salt and pepper to taste.

Toreador Crêpes
Melt 25 g/1 oz (2 tablespoons) of butter in a frying pan (skillet), add 1 onion, chopped and fry until softened. Add 1 × 225 g/8 oz can of corned beef, chopped, and cook for 2 minutes. Fill the crêpes with the mixture. Roll up and arrange in an ovenproof dish. Cover with 1 × 300 g/10½ oz can condensed tomato soup and sprinkle with 1 small packet of crushed potato crisps (chips). Bake in a preheated moderately hot oven (190°C/375°F, Gas Mark 5) for 15 to 20 minutes.

Salmon Chowder

METRIC/IMPERIAL
600 ml/1 pint milk
1 × 200 g/7 oz can sweet corn
1 × 350 g/12 oz can salmon, flaked
25 g/1 oz butter
salt and pepper
1 tablespoon chopped parsley

AMERICAN
2½ cups milk
1 × 7 oz can corn kernels
1 × ¾ lb can salmon, flaked
2 tablespoons butter
salt and pepper
1 tablespoon chopped parsley

Put the milk and corn into a pan and bring almost to the boil. Add the flaked salmon, butter, salt and pepper to taste and parsley. Heat gently for a few minutes.

Tacos

METRIC/IMPERIAL
1 kg/2 lb lean minced beef
2 envelopes taco seasoning mix
12–16 taco shells (or more)
To serve:
bottled taco sauce
grated cheese
shredded lettuce
finely chopped tomatoes
soured cream (optional)

AMERICAN
2 lb lean ground beef
2 envelopes taco seasoning mix
12–16 taco shells (or more)
To serve:
bottled taco sauce
grated cheese
shredded lettuce
finely chopped tomatoes
sour cream (optional)

Brown the beef in a dry frying pan (skillet). Sprinkle over the taco seasoning mix and stir in the quantity of water directed on the envelope. Bring to the boil and simmer for 20 minutes. Meanwhile, heat the taco shells as directed on the packet.

To serve, put a portion of meat in a taco shell and top with a little taco sauce. Add cheese, lettuce, tomatoes and sour cream, if liked.

Chilli Burgers

METRIC/IMPERIAL
8 frozen beefburgers
225 g/8 oz Gouda cheese, grated
1 × 200 g/7 oz can sweetcorn, drained
2 dessert apples, cored and chopped
2 teaspoons chilli sauce
salt and pepper
4 soft rolls, cut in half

AMERICAN
8 frozen hamburgers
2 cups grated Gouda cheese
1 × 7 oz can corn kernels, drained
2 dessert apples, cored and chopped
2 teaspoons chili sauce
salt and pepper
4 hamburger buns, cut in half

Grill (broil) the burgers on both sides. Mix together the cheese, sweetcorn (corn kernels), apples, chilli sauce and salt and pepper to taste. Toast the rolls (buns) under the grill (broiler).

Place a burger on each roll (bun) half and top with the sweetcorn (corn kernels) mixture. Grill (broil) until golden.

Lamburgers

METRIC/IMPERIAL
25 g/1 oz butter
1 onion, chopped
500 g/1 lb minced lamb
1 stick celery, chopped
1 tablespoon tomato purée
1 tablespoon tomato ketchup
1 teaspoon dried mixed herbs
salt and pepper
50 g/2 oz fresh white bread crumbs
oil for frying
To serve:
4 soft rolls, split
fried onion rings
tomato slices
lettuce leaves

AMERICAN
2 tablespoons butter
1 onion, chopped
1 lb ground lamb
1 stalk celery, chopped
1 tablespoon tomato paste
1 tablespoon tomato catsup
1 teaspoon dried mixed herbs
salt and pepper
1 cup fresh white bread crumbs
oil for frying
To serve:
4 hamburger buns, split
fried onion rings
tomato slices
lettuce leaves

Melt the butter in a frying pan (skillet), add the onion and fry until tender. Tip the onion into a bowl and mix in the lamb, celery, tomato purée (paste), ketchup (catsup), herbs, salt and pepper to taste and bread crumbs.

Divide the mixture into 4 and shape into patties. Fry in oil for about 15 minutes, turning once. Serve in split rolls (buns) with onion rings, tomato slices and lettuce leaves.

LAMBURGERS
(Photograph: New Zealand Lamb)

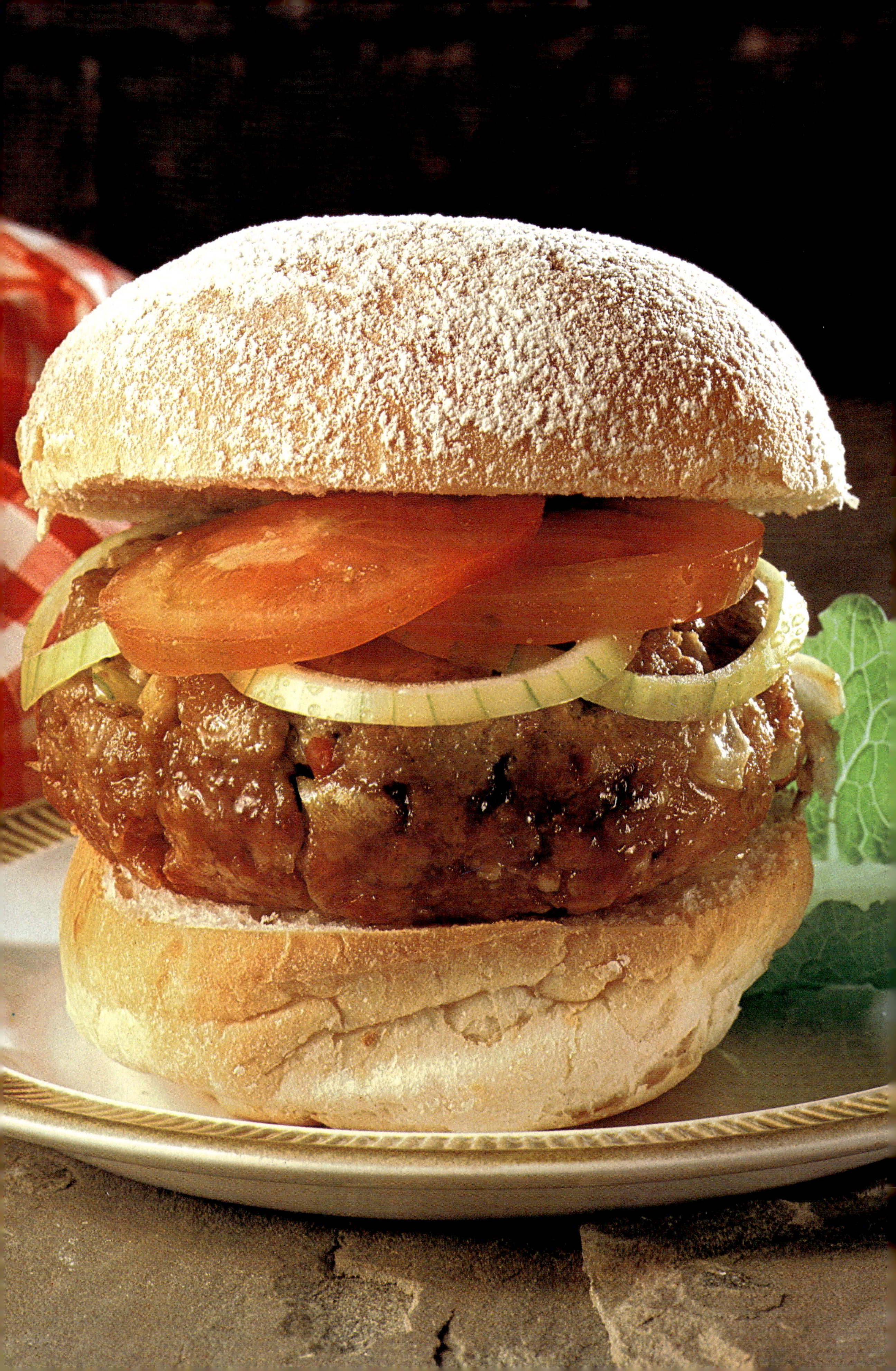

WHAT'S IN THE CUPBOARD?

Barbecued Pork with Pineapple

METRIC/IMPERIAL
4 pork chops
175 ml/6 fl oz canned or bottled barbecue sauce
4 pineapple rings

AMERICAN
4 pork chops
¾ cup canned or bottled barbecue sauce
4 pineapple rings

Place the chops in a shallow flameproof dish. Grill (broil) for about 3 minutes on each side or until browned. Drain off the fat thoroughly. Pour the sauce over the chops and continue to cook for a further 5 minutes, basting well, or until the chops are cooked through. Place a pineapple ring on each chop and cook for a final 5 minutes.

Quick Chilli con Carne

METRIC/IMPERIAL
2 teaspoons oil
1 onion, chopped
2 teaspoons chilli powder
1 × 425 g/15 oz can minced beef in gravy
1 × 447 g/15¾ oz can baked beans

AMERICAN
2 teaspoons oil
1 onion, chopped
2 teaspoons chili powder
1 × 15 oz can ground beef, in gravy
1 × 15¾ oz can baked beans

Heat the oil in a saucepan, add the onion and fry until softened. Stir in the chilli powder and cook gently for 5 minutes. Add the meat and beans and heat through. Serve with rice and salad.

Potato Pizza

METRIC/IMPERIAL
1 large packet instant mashed potato granules
1 teaspoon mixed herbs
4 tomatoes, sliced
225 g/8 oz cooked chicken meat, chopped
salt and pepper
100 g/4 oz cheese, grated
4 tablespoons cranberry sauce

AMERICAN
1 cup instant mashed potato granules
1 teaspoon mixed herbs
4 tomatoes, sliced
1 cup chopped cooked chicken meat
salt and pepper
1 cup grated cheese
¼ cup cranberry sauce

Mix the potato granules with the herbs and make up according to the instructions on the packet. Spread the potato on a greased ovenproof plate. Cover with the tomatoes and chicken and season well with salt and pepper. Sprinkle with the cheese and finish with spoonfuls of cranberry sauce. Bake in a preheated moderately hot oven (200°C/400°F, Gas Mark 6) for 15 minutes.

Chicken and Mushrooms in Potato Nests

METRIC/IMPERIAL
1 medium packet instant potato powder
25 g/1 oz butter
salt and pepper
1 × 138 g/5 oz can chicken in white sauce
1 × 213 g/7½ oz can mushrooms, drained and sliced
chopped parsley to garnish

AMERICAN
1 medium package instant potato powder
2 tablespoons butter
salt and pepper
1 × 5 oz can chicken in white sauce
1 × 7½ oz can mushrooms, drained and sliced
chopped parsley to garnish

Mix potato as directed on the packet, add butter and salt and pepper to taste. Pile potato on a greased tray and shape into nests with a fork. Fill centres with chicken and mushrooms. Heat in a moderately hot oven (200°C/400°F, Gas Mark 6) for 15 minutes. Serve hot garnished with parsley.

Panhandle Corned Beef Hash

METRIC/IMPERIAL
50 g/2 oz lard
1 onion, chopped
2 cooking apples, peeled, cored and chopped
1 × 350 g/12 oz can corned beef, chopped
225 g/8 oz potatoes, cooked and diced
2 teaspoons chopped parsley
salt and pepper
Worcestershire sauce

AMERICAN
¼ cup shortening
1 onion, chopped
2 baking apples, peeled, cored and chopped
1 × ¾ lb can corned beef, chopped
2½ cups chopped cooked potatoes
2 teaspoons chopped parsley
salt and pepper
Worcestershire sauce

Melt the lard (shortening) in a frying pan (skillet), add the onion and fry until softened. Stir in the remaining ingredients, with salt, pepper and Worcestershire sauce to taste, and press to a flat cake. Fry until crisp underneath.

To turn the cake invert onto a greased plate and slide back into the frying pan. Brown the other side. Alternatively, brown the top under the grill (broiler). Serve with a green salad.

Barbecue Butter (Baby Lima) Beans

METRIC/IMPERIAL
2 tablespoons oil
1 onion, chopped
1 garlic clove, crushed
2 tomatoes, skinned
2 teaspoons brown sugar
pinch of dry mustard
pinch of chilli powder
1 tablespoon tomato ketchup
1 × 275 g/10 oz can butter beans, drained

AMERICAN
2 tablespoons oil
1 onion, chopped
1 garlic clove, crushed
2 tomatoes, skinned
2 teaspoons brown sugar
pinch of dry mustard
pinch of chili powder
1 tablespoon tomato catsup
1 × 10 oz can baby lima beans, drained

Heat the oil in a saucepan, add the onion and garlic and fry until softened. Add the remaining ingredients, except the beans, and simmer for 10 minutes. Stir in the beans and heat thoroughly.

PANHANDLE CORNED BEEF HASH
(Photograph: The Apple and Pear Development Council)

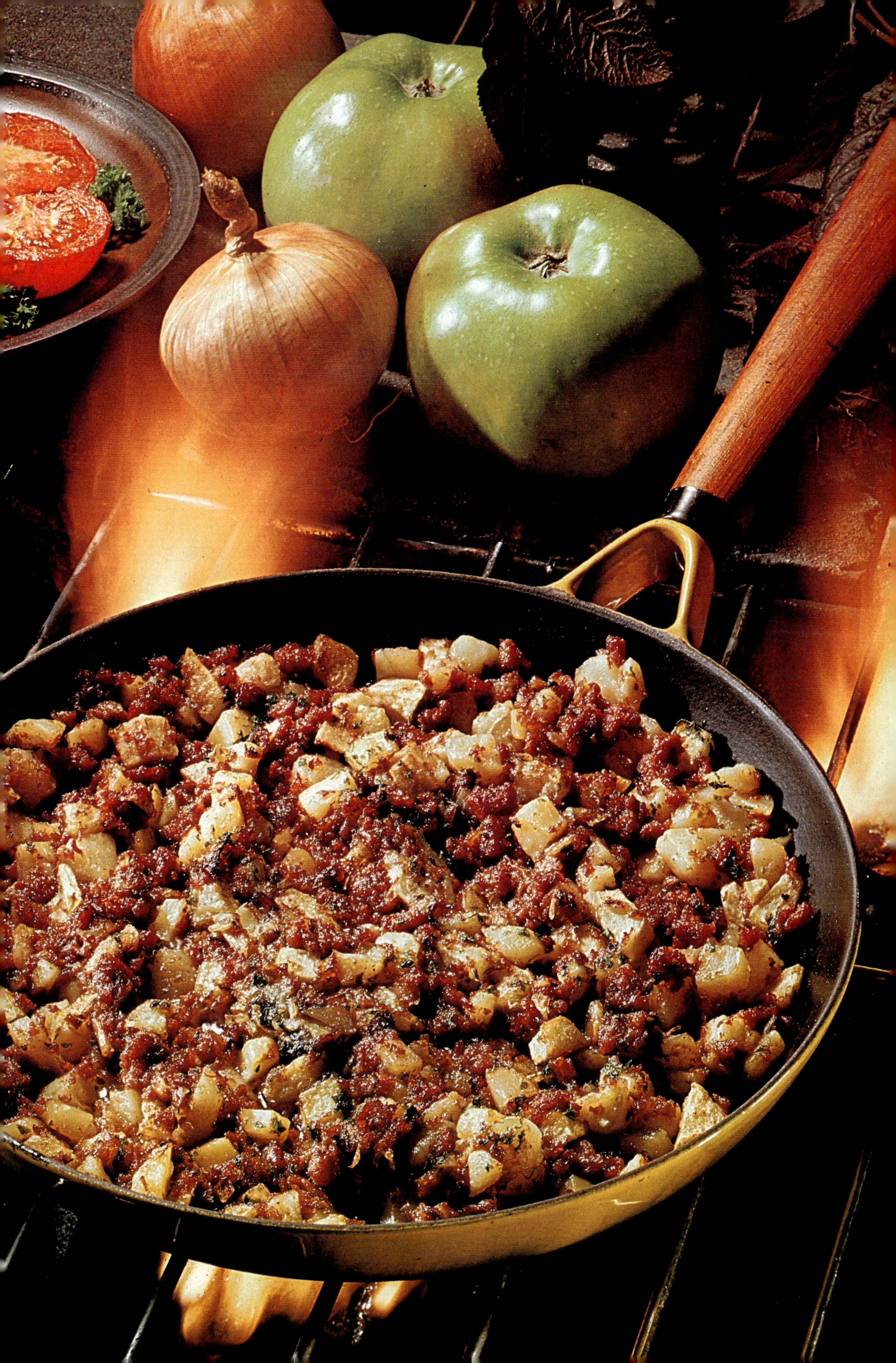

Moussaka

METRIC/IMPERIAL
75 g/3 oz margarine
225 g/½ lb potatoes, peeled and grated
225 g/½ lb onions, peeled and grated
1 × 500 g/1 lb can stewed steak
Sauce:
25 g/1 oz flour
300 ml/½ pint milk
25 g/1 oz butter
75 g/3 oz Cheddar cheese, grated
salt and pepper
Garnish:
grated nutmeg

AMERICAN
6 tablespoons margarine
2⅓ cups peeled and grated potatoes
2 cups peeled and grated onions
1 × 1 lb can stewed steak
Sauce:
¼ cup flour
1⅓ cups milk
2 tablespoons butter
⅔ cup grated Cheddar cheese
salt and pepper
Garnish:
grated nutmeg

Heat the margarine in a frying pan (skillet). Add the potatoes and onions and cook for about 8 minutes until just tender. Tip the stewed steak into the pan and mix with the vegetables. Heat thoroughly.

Meanwhile make the sauce by blending the flour and milk, then tip into a saucepan, add the butter and bring to the boil, stirring until thickened. Season to taste with salt and pepper, add the grated cheese and heat until melted.

Put the meat mixture in a shallow dish, top with the sauce and garnish with nutmeg.

Speedy Beef 'n' Rice

METRIC/IMPERIAL
1 × 298 g/10½ oz can condensed oxtail soup
150 ml/¼ pint water
1 × 426 g/15 oz can minced steak and gravy
75 g/3 oz rice
2 tablespoons Worcestershire sauce
Garnish:
1 × 227 g/8 oz packet frozen peas
4 tomatoes, cut into wedges

AMERICAN
1 × 10½ oz can condensed oxtail soup
⅔ cup water
1 × 15 oz can minced steak and gravy
½ cup rice
2 tablespoons Worcestershire sauce
Garnish:
1 × ½ lb package frozen peas
4 tomatoes, cut into wedges

Place the soup, water, minced steak and rice in a saucepan. Bring to the boil stirring continuously. Simmer for 20 minutes without the lid. Cook the peas as instructed on the packet. Serve the meat mixture in a flat dish and arrange the peas and tomatoes around the edge as a garnish.

Corn and Bacon Fritters

METRIC/IMPERIAL
100 g/4 oz flour
pinch of salt
1 egg
150 ml/¼ pint milk
1 teaspoon Worcestershire sauce
225 g/8 oz frozen sweetcorn, thawed
50 g/2 oz streaky bacon rashers, rinded, fried and chopped
1 tablespoon oil
25 g/1 oz butter

AMERICAN
1 cup flour
pinch of salt
1 egg
⅔ cup milk
1 teaspoon Worcestershire sauce
½ lb frozen corn kernels, thawed
4 bacon slices, fried and chopped
1 tablespoon oil
2 tablespoons butter

Sift the flour and salt into a bowl. Beat in the egg and half the milk to form a smooth batter. Stir in the rest of the milk and the Worcestershire sauce. Add the corn and the bacon.

Heat the oil and butter in a frying pan (skillet) and drop in a tablespoonful of the batter. Fry until crisp, turning once.
Makes about 12 fritters.

SANDWICHES HOT AND COLD

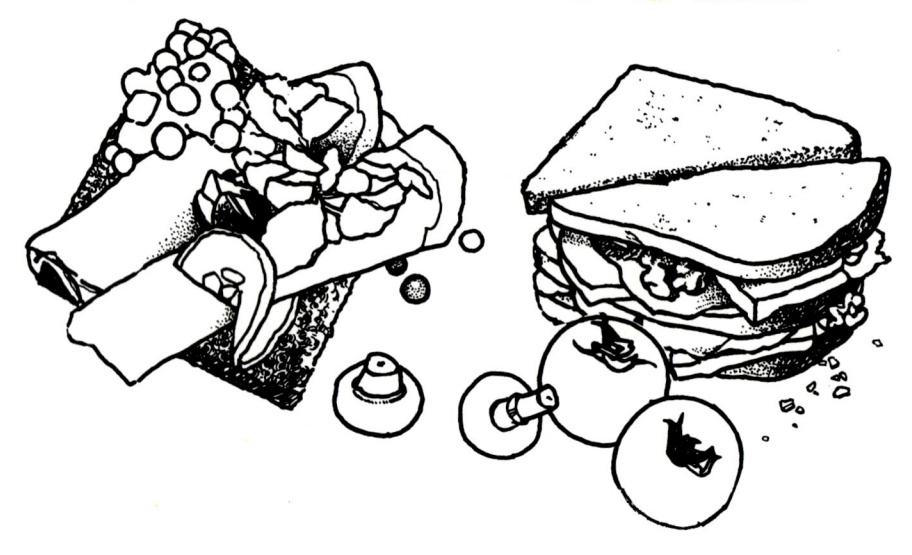

Fried Silverside (Corned Beef) Sandwiches

METRIC/IMPERIAL
25 g/1 oz butter
8 large slices of white bread
4 tablespoons sweet pickle
4 slices of cooked beef silverside
2 eggs, beaten
75 ml/3 fl oz milk
pepper
oil for shallow frying
mustard and cress to garnish

AMERICAN
2 tablespoons butter
8 large slices of white bread
$\frac{1}{4}$ cup pickle relish
4 slices of corned beef
2 eggs, beaten
6 tablespoons milk
pepper
oil for shallow frying
garden cress to garnish

Butter the slices of bread and spread with the pickle (relish). Lay the beef on four of the bread slices and cover with the remaining slices. Press gently together, then cut each sandwich in half diagonally to make two triangles.

Beat the eggs with the milk and pepper to taste. Dip the sandwiches in the egg mixture to coat well all over.

Heat a little oil in a frying pan (skillet), add the sandwiches, in batches, and fry until golden brown on both sides. Serve hot, garnished with cress.

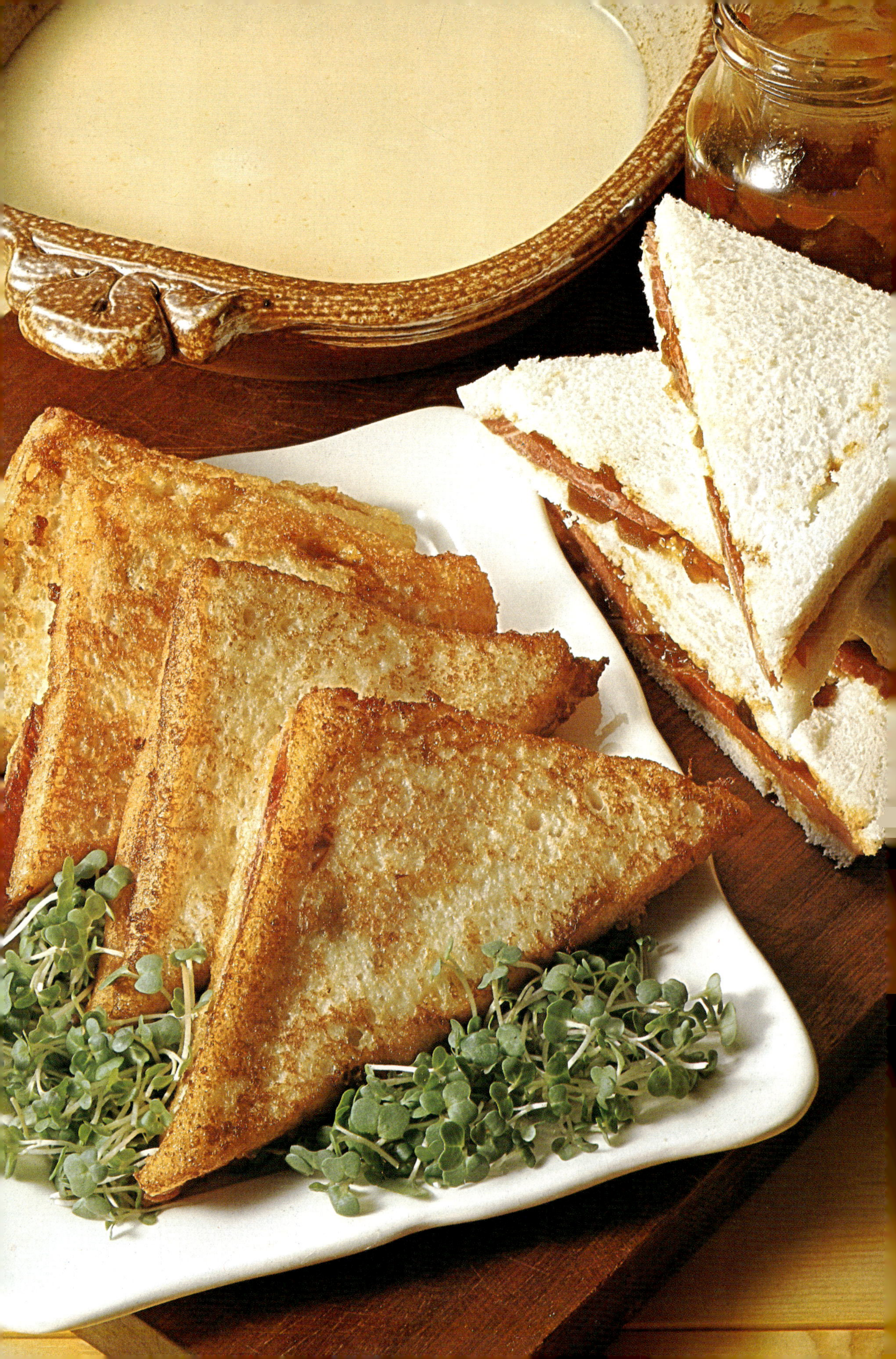

Sardine Toasties

METRIC/IMPERIAL
1 × 225 g/8 oz can tomatoes
salt and pepper
4 slices bread
butter
1 × 100 g/4 oz can sardines, drained
  and mashed
Garnish:
anchovy fillets
black olives

AMERICAN
1 × 8 oz can tomatoes
salt and pepper
4 slices bread
butter
1 × 4 oz can sardines, drained
  and mashed
Garnish:
anchovy fillets
ripe olives

Pour the tomatoes into a pan, add salt and pepper and simmer until the tomatoes form a thick pulp. Toast the bread, spread with butter then with the sardines. Grill (broil) for a few minutes. Top with the tomato pulp and garnish with anchovy fillets and olives.

Crab and Tomato Toasts

METRIC/IMPERIAL
4 slices bread
50 g/2 oz butter
1 × 200 g/7 oz can crab meat
juice of ½ lemon
1 tablespoon tomato purée
salt and pepper
Garnish:
4 lemon wedges
watercress

AMERICAN
4 slices bread
4 tablespoons (½ stick) butter
1 × 7 oz can crab meat
juice of ½ lemon
1 tablespoon tomato paste
salt and pepper
Garnish:
4 lemon wedges
watercress

Toast the bread and spread with 25 g/1 oz (2 tablespoons) of the butter. Blend the crab meat with the remaining butter, lemon juice and purée (paste). Season with salt and pepper and spread onto the hot toast. Heat for a few minutes then serve garnished with lemon wedges and watercress.

Devilled Sausage Toppers

METRIC/IMPERIAL
100 g/4 oz Cheddar cheese, grated
1 teaspoon prepared mustard
1 teaspoon Worcestershire sauce
pinch of cayenne pepper
salt
8 chipolata sausages
4 slices of bread
50 g/2 oz butter
4 tomatoes, sliced
parsley to garnish

AMERICAN
1 cup grated Cheddar cheese
1 teaspoon prepared mustard
1 teaspoon Worcestershire sauce
pinch of cayenne pepper
salt
8 link sausages
4 slices of bread
4 tablespoons butter
4 tomatoes, sliced
parsley to garnish

Mix together the cheese, mustard, Worcestershire sauce, cayenne and salt to taste. Grill (broil) the sausages, and toast the bread. Butter the toast and top with the sausages, then the tomatoes and cheese mixture. Grill (broil) for 2 to 3 minutes. Garnish with parsley.

Corn and Bacon Rolls

METRIC/IMPERIAL
4 brown rolls
300 ml/½ pint milk
25 g/1 oz butter
25 g/1 oz flour
50 g/2 oz Cheddar cheese, grated
100 g/4 oz canned sweetcorn
4 smoked bacon rashers, rinded, grilled and chopped
½ red pepper, cored, seeded and chopped
salt and pepper

AMERICAN
4 brown rolls
1¼ cups milk
2 tablespoons butter
¼ cup flour
½ cup grated Cheddar cheese
¾ cup canned corn kernels
4 bacon slices, broiled and chopped
½ red pepper, cored, seeded and chopped
salt and pepper

Cut the tops off the rolls and scoop out the centres. Melt the butter in a saucepan, stir in the flour and cook for 1 minute. Gradually stir in the milk and bring to the boil. Simmer until thickened. Stir in the cheese, corn, bacon, red pepper and salt and pepper to taste.

Place spoonfuls of the mixture in the hollowed-out rolls and replace the lids. Bake in a preheated moderate oven (180°C/350°F, Gas Mark 4) for 5 to 10 minutes.

Regal Toasts

METRIC/IMPERIAL
50 g/2 oz butter
500 g/1 lb mushrooms, sliced
50 g/2 oz split almonds
1 tablespoon soy sauce
2 drops Angostura bitters
salt and pepper
2 tablespoons double cream
1 tablespoon chopped parsley
4 slices hot buttered toast

AMERICAN
4 tablespoons butter
1 lb mushrooms, sliced
⅓ cup split almonds
1 tablespoon soy sauce
2 drops Angostura bitters
salt and pepper
2 tablespoons heavy cream
1 tablespoon chopped parsley
4 slices hot buttered toast

Melt the butter in a frying pan (skillet), add the mushrooms and almonds and fry lightly. Add the soy sauce and Angostura bitters. Season to taste with salt and pepper. Cook for about 3 minutes, until most of the liquid has evaporated. Remove from the heat and stir in the cream and parsley. Serve on the toast.

Jubilee Toasts

METRIC/IMPERIAL
50 g/2 oz butter
500 g/1 lb open mushrooms
salt and pepper
lemon juice
4 slices of buttered toast

AMERICAN
4 tablespoons butter
1 lb flat mushrooms
salt and pepper
lemon juice
4 slices of buttered toast

Melt the butter in the grill (broiler) pan and dip in the mushrooms. Grill (broil) for 2 minutes. Turn the mushrooms over and season with salt, pepper and a little lemon juice. Cook for a further 2 minutes. Serve on hot buttered toast.

JUBILEE TOASTS
(Photograph: Mushroom Growers' Association)

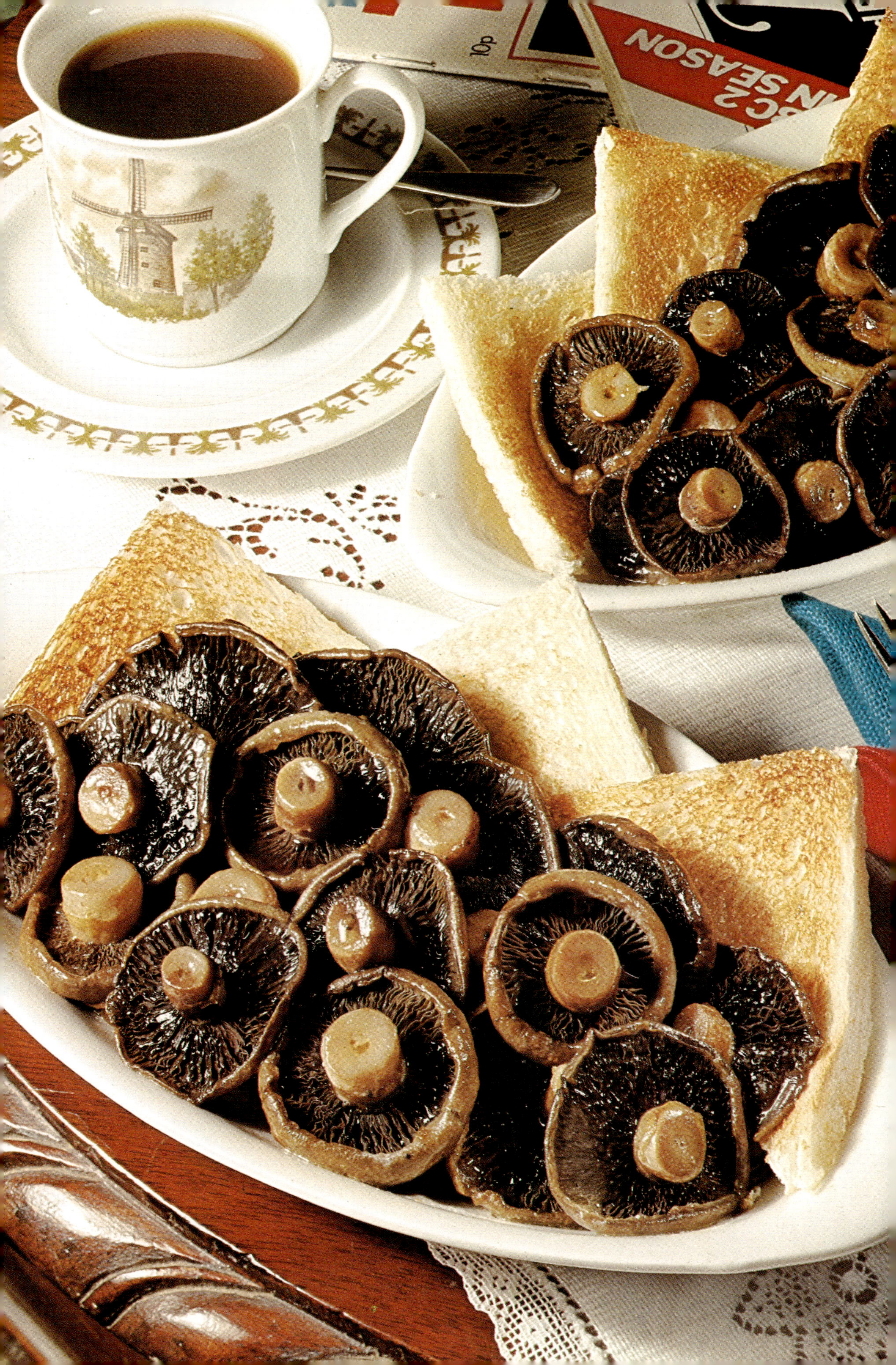
10p
BC 2
IN SEASON

Club Sandwich

METRIC/IMPERIAL
slices of brown and white bread, lightly toasted
butter
salt and pepper
Suggested fillings:
slices of roast beef and lettuce
slices of salami and watercress
prawn mayonnaise
chopped cooked chicken and chopped tomato
slices of cooked ham and fruit chutney
Garnish:
radishes
parsley sprigs

AMERICAN
slices of brown and white bread, lightly toasted
butter
salt and pepper
Suggested fillings:
slices of roast beef and lettuce
slices of salami and watercress
shrimp mayonnaise
chopped cooked chicken and chopped tomato
slices of cooked ham and fruit chutney
Garnish:
radishes
parsley sprigs

This is a layered sandwich with a different filling between each layer. Select fillings from the suggestions above and decide the number of layers you wish to have. Butter the toast and cut in half diagonally. Then build up the sandwich layers using alternate triangles of brown and white toast with the selected fillings in between. Season each filling with salt and pepper to taste. Decorate the top toast layer with a radish and a sprig of parsley.

Egg and Mushroom Rarebit

METRIC/IMPERIAL
4 slices of bread
50 g/2 oz butter
100 g/4 oz mushrooms, sliced
salt and pepper
8 eggs
1 tablespoon beer or cider
100 g/4 oz cheese, grated
½ teaspoon prepared mustard

AMERICAN
4 slices of bread
4 tablespoons butter
1 cup sliced mushrooms
salt and pepper
8 eggs
1 tablespoon beer or hard cider
1 cup grated cheese
½ teaspoon prepared mustard

Cut the bread into triangles. Melt 25 g/1 oz (2 tablespoons) of the butter in a frying pan (skillet) and fry the bread until crisp on one side only. Arrange, fried side down, in a baking dish. Arrange the mushrooms over the bread and season with salt and pepper. Break the eggs on top of the mushrooms. Melt the rest of the butter in a saucepan and remove from the heat. Stir in the beer or cider, cheese and mustard. Spoon the mixture over the eggs. Bake in a preheated hot oven (220°C/425°F, Gas Mark 7) for 20 minutes. Serve hot with vegetables.

Toasted Bacon and Mushroom Sandwich

METRIC/IMPERIAL
25 g/1 oz butter
8 streaky bacon rashers, rinded and chopped
225 g/8 oz mushrooms, sliced
1 teaspoon dried mixed herbs
salt and pepper
2 eggs, beaten
8 slices of buttered bread

AMERICAN
2 tablespoons butter
8 bacon slices, chopped
2 cups sliced mushrooms
1 teaspoon dried mixed herbs
salt and pepper
2 eggs, beaten
8 slices of buttered bread

Melt the butter in a frying pan (skillet), add the bacon and mushrooms and fry until golden. Stir in the herbs and salt and pepper to taste. Pour in the eggs and cook until lightly set. Spread the mixture onto four of the bread slices and top with the remaining bread, buttered sides in. Toast the sandwiches until they are golden brown.

Egg and Celery Loaf

METRIC/IMPERIAL
4 small French loaves
175 g/6 oz butter
10 eggs
salt and pepper
6 sticks celery, finely chopped
2 large tomatoes, skinned and chopped
2 tablespoons mayonnaise (see page 42)
1 tablespoon chutney
shredded lettuce leaves

AMERICAN
4 small French loaves
12 tablespoons (1½ sticks) butter
10 eggs
salt and pepper
6 stalks celery, finely chopped
2 large tomatoes, skinned and chopped
2 tablespoons mayonnaise (see page 42)
1 tablespoon chutney
shredded lettuce leaves

Split the loaves and spread with 100 g/4 oz (8 tablespoons) of the butter. Beat the eggs with salt and pepper to taste. Melt the remaining butter in a saucepan, add the eggs and cook gently until lightly scrambled. Allow to cool. Mix the celery, tomatoes, mayonnaise and chutney into the eggs. Fill the loaves with lettuce and the egg mixture.

Alternative fillings:
Scrambled egg with watercress, chopped gherkins and cucumber, grated raw carrot, grated cooked beetroot (beets), shredded chicory (Belgian endive), spring onions (scallions), pickles (relish), chutney, ketchup (catsup), meat extract and savoury pastes.

Danish Open Sandwiches

A quick and easy way to entertain is to present a selection of cold meats, cheese, vegetables and garnishes and leave your guests to make up their own open sandwiches. If you decide to prepare the sandwiches yourself, ahead of time, there is still no last-minute cooking to be done.

The base of the sandwich should be a firm bread, such as pumpernickel, or a crispbread, spread with butter so the bread does not become soggy, and topped with a lettuce leaf.

A selection of toppings could include: slices of salami, slices of cooked ham, slices of pâté, sliced or grated cheese, slices of hard-boiled (hard-cooked) egg, rollmops or other pickled fish, caviar or lumpfish roe, cooked vegetables such as mushrooms and peas, crisply fried bacon, onion rings, sliced radishes and cucumber and tomato strips. Garnishes such as parsley sprigs, mustard and cress (garden cress), lemon slices, and clusters of grapes, as well as mayonnaise and mustards, will provide the finishing touches.

Cheese Double Deckers

METRIC/IMPERIAL	AMERICAN
225 g/8 oz Edam cheese	*½ lb Edam cheese*
4 crisp rolls	*4 crisp rolls*
100 g/4 oz butter	*8 tablespoons (1 stick) butter*
8 lettuce leaves	*8 lettuce leaves*
2 tomatoes, sliced	*2 tomatoes, sliced*
4 tablespoons tomato pickle	*¼ cup tomato relish*
cucumber slices	*cucumber slices*

Cut half the cheese into four slices and grate the remainder. Make two cuts diagonally almost through each roll. Butter one side of each cut. Put half of the lettuce, the tomatoes and pickle (relish) and slices of Edam in one cut. Put the remaining lettuce, the cucumber and grated Edam in the second cut.

CHEESE DOUBLE DECKERS
(*Photograph: Dutch Dairy Bureau*)

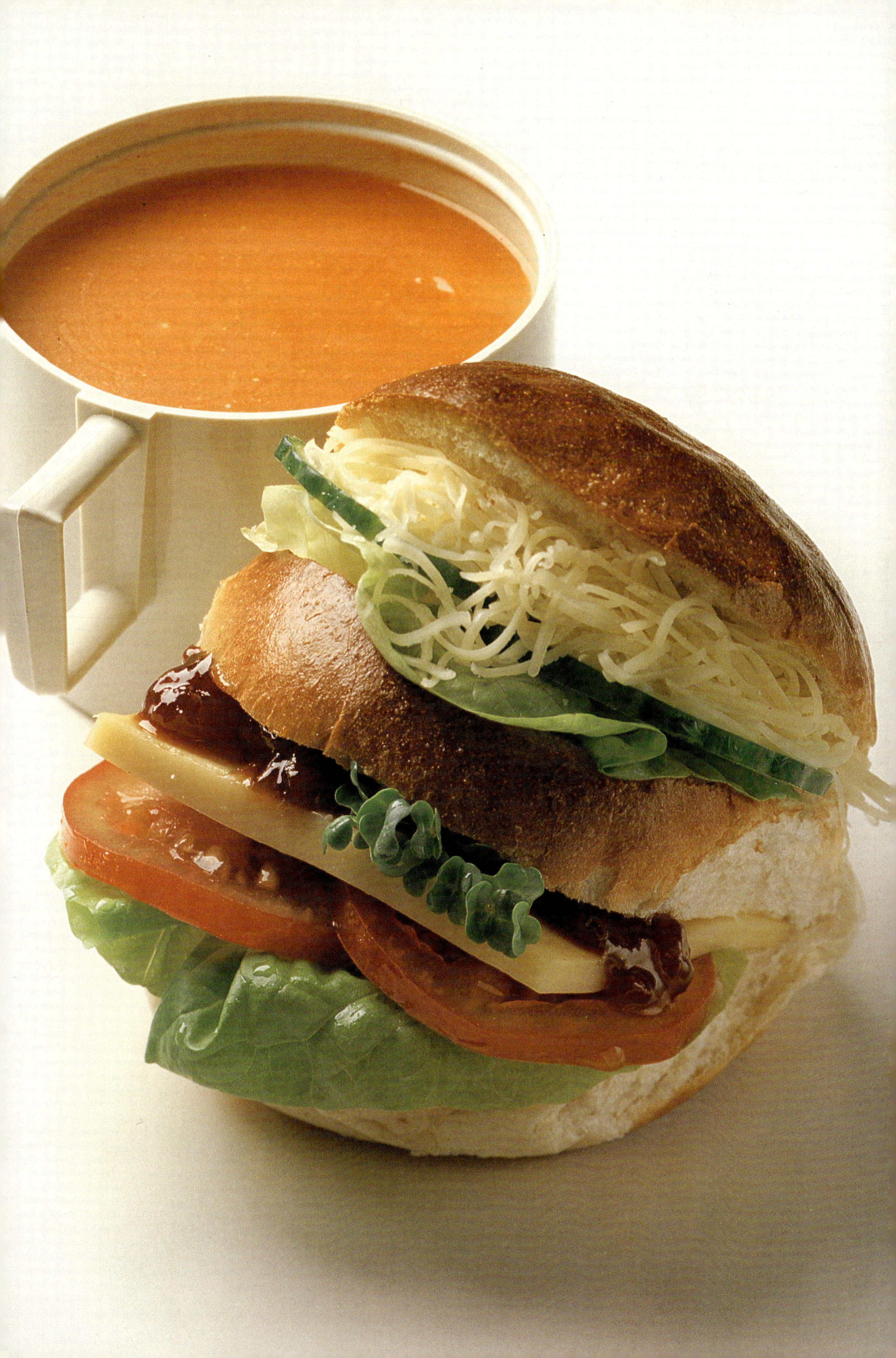

SPEEDY SALADS

Mayonnaise

METRIC/IMPERIAL
1 egg yolk
½ teaspoon dry mustard
salt and pepper
½ teaspoon sugar
150 ml/¼ pint salad oil
1 tablespoon white wine vinegar
  or lemon juice

AMERICAN
1 egg yolk
½ teaspoon dry mustard
salt and pepper
½ teaspoon sugar
⅔ cup salad oil
1 tablespoon white wine vinegar
  or lemon juice

Put the egg yolk, mustard, salt, pepper and sugar in a bowl. Mix thoroughly then add the oil, a drop at a time, stirring constantly. When the sauce is thick and smooth add the vinegar or lemon juice gradually and mix thoroughly.

French Dressing

METRIC/IMPERIAL
3 tablespoons salad oil
¼ teaspoon dry mustard
½ teaspoon sugar
1½ tablespoons vinegar
salt and pepper

AMERICAN
3 tablespoons salad oil
¼ teaspoon dry mustard
½ teaspoon sugar
1½ tablespoons vinegar
salt and pepper

Put all the ingredients in a screw-topped jar and shake thoroughly.

Continental Salad

METRIC/IMPERIAL
1 green pepper, cored, seeded and sliced
2 sticks celery, sliced
1 large carrot, sliced
1 onion, chopped
1 × 500 g/1 lb 3 oz can new potatoes, drained
100 g/4 oz salami slices
100 g/4 oz cooked chicken meat, chopped
1 quantity French dressing (see opposite)

AMERICAN
1 green pepper, cored, seeded and sliced
2 stalks celery, sliced
1 large carrot, sliced
1 onion, chopped
1 × 1 lb 3 oz can new potatoes, drained
¼ lb salami slices
½ cup chopped cooked chicken meat
1 quantity French dressing (see opposite)

Mix together the green pepper, celery, carrot, onion, potatoes, salami and chicken in a salad bowl. Pour the dressing over the salad and toss well.

Devilled Potato and Chicken Salad

METRIC/IMPERIAL
750 g/1½ lb potatoes
6 frankfurter sausages, cooked and chopped
175 g/6 oz cooked chicken meat, chopped
150 ml/¼ pint mayonnaise (see opposite)
1 bunch spring onions, chopped

AMERICAN
1½ lb potatoes
6 frankfurters, cooked and chopped
1 cup chopped cooked chicken meat
⅔ cup mayonnaise (see opposite)
1 bunch scallions, chopped

Cook the potatoes in boiling water until tender, then drain and chop. Cool. Pile the potatoes, frankfurters and chicken in a dish. Mix together the mayonnaise and spring onions (scallions) and pour over the top.

Potato Salad
For potato salad follow the recipe and method above, but omit the frankfurters and chicken.

Russian Salad

METRIC/IMPERIAL
350 g/12 oz cooked chicken meat, cut into strips
1 Spanish onion, sliced thinly
2 large dill pickles, sliced thinly
2 hard-boiled eggs, sliced
550 g/1¼ lb potato salad (see page 43)
1 tablespoon capers
Garnish:
1 tomato, quartered
1 hard-boiled egg, sliced
green olives

AMERICAN
¾ lb cooked chicken meat, cut into strips
1 Bermuda onion, sliced thinly
2 large dill pickles, sliced thinly
2 hard-cooked eggs, sliced
1¼ lb potato salad (see page 43)
1 tablespoon capers
Garnish:
1 tomato, quartered
1 hard-cooked egg, sliced
green olives

Mix together the chicken, onion, pickles, eggs, potato salad and capers in a salad bowl. Garnish with the tomato, egg slices and olives.

Salad Niçoise

METRIC/IMPERIAL
350 g/12 oz canned vegetable and mayonnaise salad
275 g/10 oz canned potato salad
2 tomatoes, skinned, seeded and quartered
3 hard-boiled eggs, quartered
275 g/10 oz French beans, blanched
1 onion, sliced into rings
75 g/3 oz black olives
1 × 200 g/7 oz can tuna fish in oil, drained and flaked
6 anchovy fillets
3 tablespoons French dressing (see page 42)
2 tablespoons chopped parsley to garnish

AMERICAN
¾ lb canned vegetable and mayonnaise salad
10 oz canned potato salad
2 tomatoes, skinned, seeded and quartered
3 hard-cooked eggs, quartered
10 oz green beans, blanched
1 onion, sliced into rings
½ cup ripe olives
1 × 7 oz can tuna fish in oil, drained and flaked
6 anchovy fillets
3 tablespoons French dressing (see page 42)
2 tablespoons chopped parsley to garnish

Mix together the salads and place in the centre of a large serving dish. Toss together the tomatoes, eggs, beans, onion and olives and arrange around the mixed salads. Pile the tuna in the centre of the dish and garnish with the parsley.

RUSSIAN SALAD, WALDORF SALAD, SALAD NICOISE
(Photograph: Carmel Produce Information Bureau)

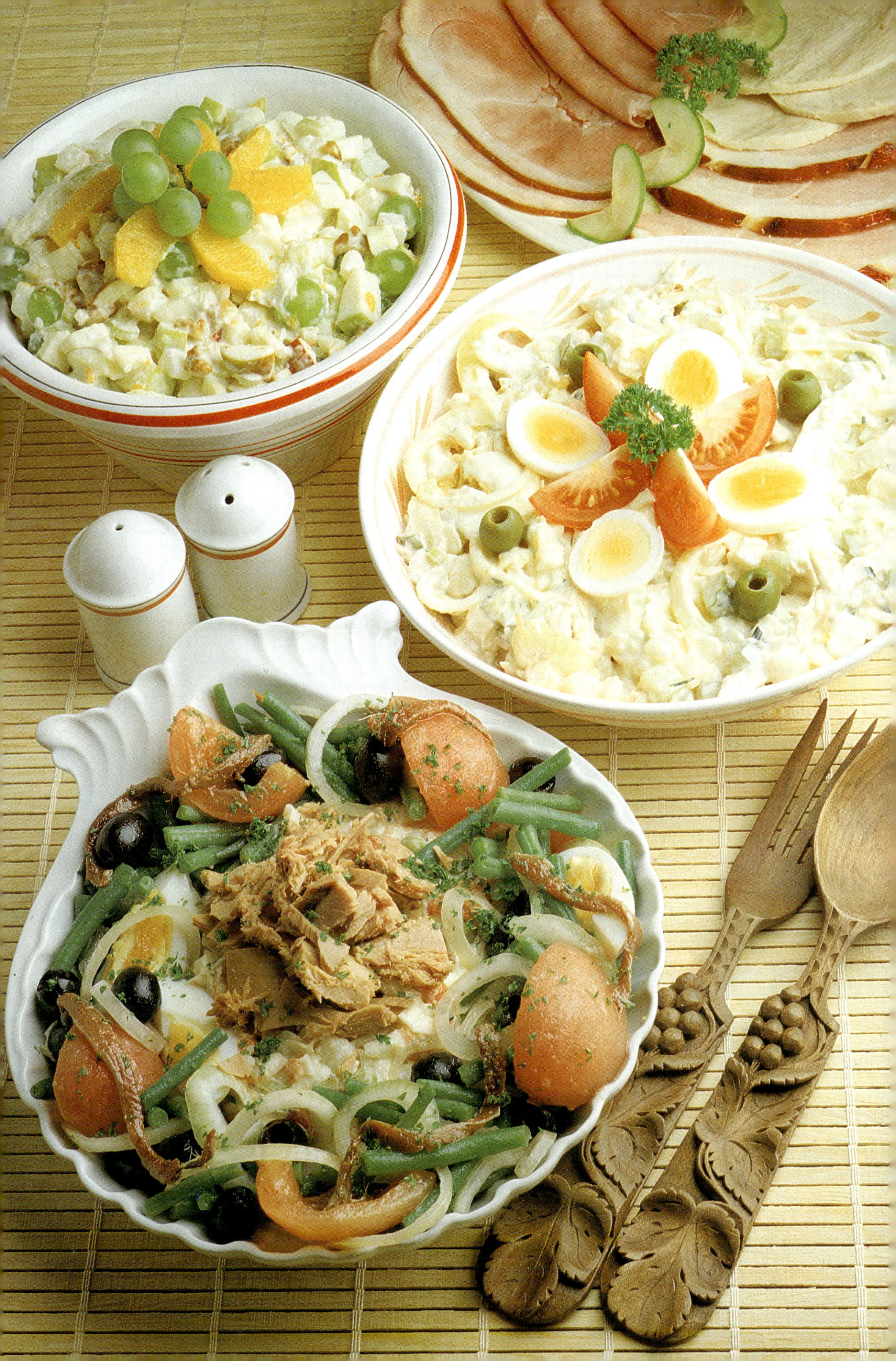

Waldorf Salad

METRIC/IMPERIAL
4–6 sticks celery, chopped
1 red dessert apple, cored and chopped
1 green dessert apple, cored and chopped
50 g/2 oz walnuts, chopped
150 ml/¼ pint mayonnaise (see page 42)
100 g/4 oz green grapes, pipped (optional)
Garnish:
orange segments
small bunch of green grapes

AMERICAN
4–6 stalks celery, chopped
1 red dessert apple, cored and chopped
1 green dessert apple, cored and chopped
½ cup chopped walnuts
⅔ cup mayonnaise (see page 42)
¼ lb white grapes, seeded (optional)
Garnish:
orange segments
small bunch of white grapes

Mix together the celery, apples, walnuts and mayonnaise in a salad bowl. Fold in the grapes, if used. Garnish with segments of orange and grapes. Serve chilled.

Crispy Duck Salad

METRIC/IMPERIAL
350 g/12 oz cold roast duck meat
2 tablespoons French dressing (see page 42)
1 tablespoon lemon juice
50 g/2 oz walnuts, chopped
4 sticks celery, chopped
1 red dessert apple, cored and diced
3 tablespoons mayonnaise (see page 42)
1 crisp lettuce, separated into leaves
12 stuffed olives
2 tomatoes, cut into wedges

AMERICAN
¾ lb cold roast duck meat
2 tablespoons French dressing (see page 42)
1 tablespoon lemon juice
½ cup chopped walnuts
4 stalks celery, chopped
1 red dessert apple, cored and chopped finely
3 tablespoons mayonnaise (see page 42)
1 crisp head of lettuce, separated into leaves
12 stuffed olives
2 tomatoes, cut into wedges

Remove the duck skin and reserve. Cut the meat into strips and toss in the French dressing and lemon juice. Leave to marinate for 1 hour, if possible.

Grill (broil) the skin until very crisp. Mix together the walnuts, celery, apple and mayonnaise and stir in the meat strips. Place the lettuce in a salad bowl and pile the meat salad on top. Chop the crisp skin and sprinkle on top. Garnish with the olives and tomatoes.

King Camembert Salad

METRIC/IMPERIAL
1 Savoy cabbage, cored and finely shredded
225 g/8 oz Camembert, cubed
100 g/4 oz peanuts
100 g/4 oz sultanas
150 ml/¼ pint French dressing (see page 42)

AMERICAN
1 head of Savoy cabbage, cored and finely shredded
½ lb Camembert, cubed
½ cup peanuts
⅔ cup seedless white raisins
⅔ cup French dressing (see page 42)

Toss all the ingredients together in a salad bowl.

Slimmer's Delight

METRIC/IMPERIAL
150 ml/¼ pint natural yogurt
1 tablespoon tomato purée
1 tablespoon chopped chives or spring onions
salt and pepper
225 g/8 oz button mushrooms
chicory leaves

AMERICAN
⅔ cup unflavored yogurt
1 tablespoon tomato paste
1 tablespoon chopped chives or scallions
salt and pepper
2 cups button mushrooms
Belgian endive leaves

Mix together the yogurt, tomato purée (paste), chives or spring onions (scallions) and salt and pepper to taste. Stir in the mushrooms and serve on a bed of chicory (endive) leaves.

Mixed Bean Salad

METRIC/IMPERIAL
1 × 432 g/15¼ oz can red kidney beans
1 × 425 g/15 oz can broad beans
1 × 439 g/15½ oz can butter beans or baked beans
100 g/4 oz cabbage, cored and finely shredded, or bean sprouts
salt and pepper
6 tablespoons French dressing (see page 42)

AMERICAN
1 × 15¼ oz can red kidney beans
1 × 15 oz can lima beans
1 × 15½ oz can baby lima or baked beans
1¼ cups finely shredded cabbage or bean sprouts
salt and pepper
6 tablespoons French dressing (see page 42)

Drain all the beans, retaining the liquid for use in a soup or gravy. Turn the mixed beans into a bowl, add the cabbage or bean sprouts and season to taste with salt and pepper. Toss in the French dressing. Serve chilled.

SIMPLE SUPPERS

Chicken and Chestnut Soup

METRIC/IMPERIAL
1 × 440 g/15½ oz can whole chestnuts in water, drained and chopped
1 × 425 g/15 oz can cream of chicken soup
1 tablespoon dry sherry
grated rind of 1 orange
1 tablespoon single cream

AMERICAN
1 × 15½ oz can whole chestnuts in water, drained and chopped
1 × 15 oz can cream of chicken soup
1 tablespoon dry sherry
grated rind of 1 orange
1 tablespoon light cream

Put the chestnuts, soup, sherry and orange rind in a saucepan and heat gently without boiling. Stir in the cream just before serving.

Isle of Skye Soup

METRIC/IMPERIAL
2 × 300 g/11½ oz cans condensed cream of mushroom soup
milk
3 tablespoons whisky
3 tablespoons single cream
4 button mushrooms, sliced to garnish

AMERICAN
2 × 11½ oz cans condensed cream of mushroom soup
milk
3 tablespoons whisky
3 tablespoons light cream
4 button mushrooms, sliced to garnish

Make up the soup with the milk as directed on the can and heat in a saucepan. Put the whisky into warmed soup bowls, pour in the soup and swirl the cream on top. Garnish with the mushrooms.

ISLE OF SKYE SOUP
(Photograph: Mushroom Growers' Association)

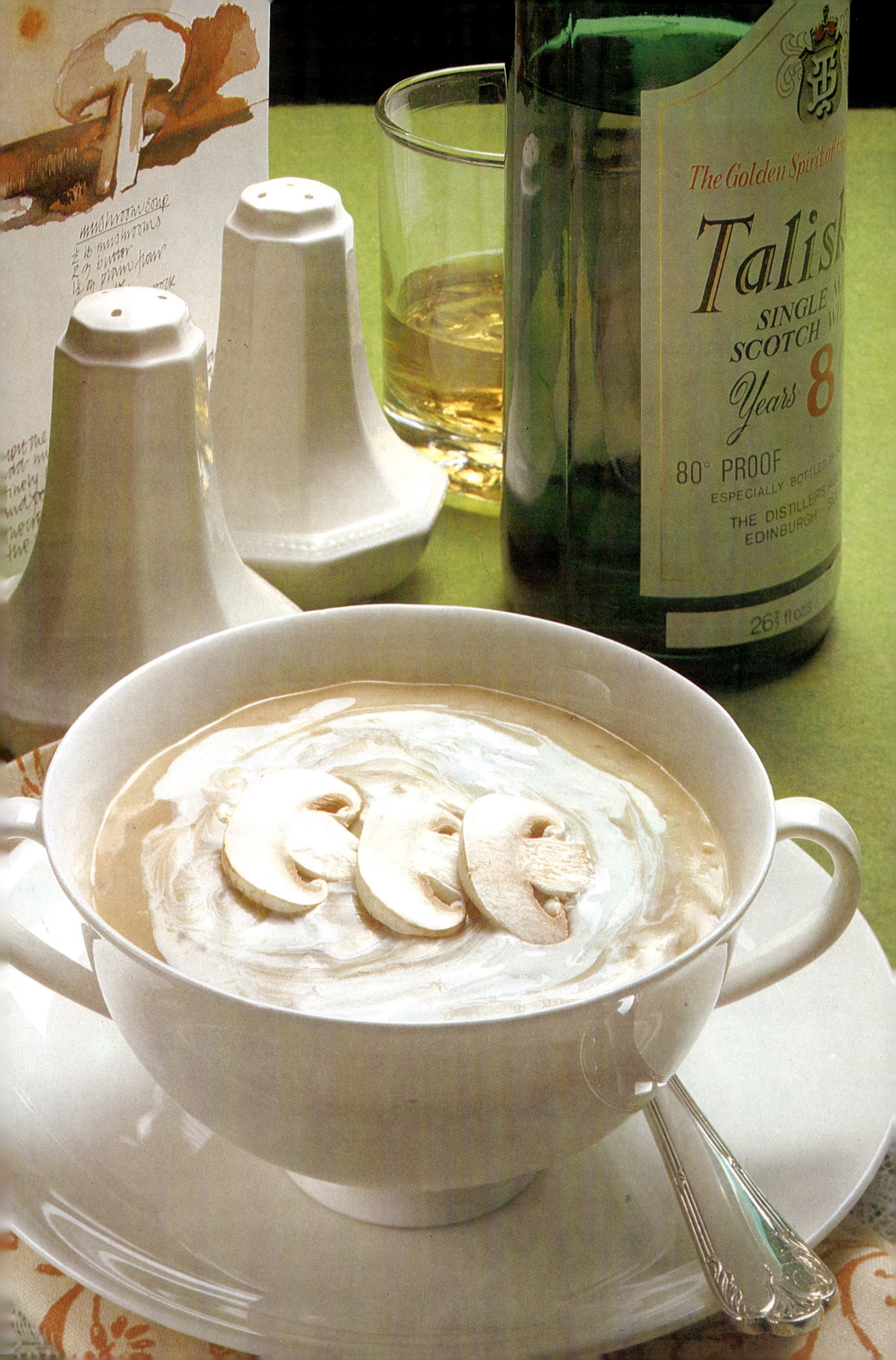
mushroom soup
SINGLE
SCOTCH
Years 8
80° PROOF
EDINBURGH

Hot Cheese Soup

METRIC/IMPERIAL
25 g/1 oz butter
1 onion, chopped
25 g/1 oz flour
600 ml/1 pint milk
300 ml/½ pint water
2 tomatoes, skinned, seeded and cut into small strips
3 tablespoons tomato purée
salt and pepper
175 g/6 oz Cheddar cheese, grated
parsley sprigs to garnish

AMERICAN
2 tablespoons butter
1 onion, chopped
¼ cup flour
2½ cups milk
1¼ cups water
2 tomatoes, skinned, seeded and cut into small strips
3 tablespoons tomato paste
salt and pepper
1½ cups grated Cheddar cheese
parsley sprigs to garnish

Melt the butter in a saucepan, add the onion and fry until softened. Stir in the flour and cook for 1 minute. Remove from the heat and gradually stir in the milk, water, tomatoes and tomato purée (paste). Return to the heat and bring to the boil, stirring. Season to taste with salt and pepper and simmer for 5 minutes. Remove from the heat and stir in the cheese until melted. Garnish with parsley.

Melon and Pineapple Dip

METRIC/IMPERIAL
1 medium melon
225 g/8 oz cream cheese
50 g/2 oz yogurt
2 teaspoons tomato purée
1 × 350 g/12 oz can pineapple chunks, drained
1 tablespoon chopped parsley
juice from the pineapple chunks
salt and pepper

AMERICAN
1 medium melon
1 cup cream cheese
3 tablespoons unflavored yogurt
2 teaspoons tomato paste
1 × 12 oz can pineapple chunks, drained
1 tablespoon chopped parsley
juice from the pineapple chunks
salt and pepper

Cut the top off the melon, remove the seeds (pits) and scoop out the flesh. Blend the cream cheese, yogurt and tomato purée (paste) until smooth. Stir in the melon flesh, the pineapple and parsley. Mix thoroughly; add a little pineapple juice if the mixture is too stiff. Season with salt and pepper to taste. Spoon the mixture back into the melon case.

Avocado Cocktail

METRIC/IMPERIAL
2 avocado pears, peeled, stoned and
  and chopped
3 tablespoons mayonnaise (see
  page 42)
1 × 200 g/7 oz can crab meat
1 green pepper, cored, seeded and
  chopped
salt and pepper
4 lettuce leaves, shredded
4 lemon wedges

AMERICAN
2 avocado pears, peeled, pitted and
  chopped
3 tablespoons mayonnaise (see
  page 42)
1 × 7 oz can crab meat
1 green pepper, cored, seeded and
  chopped
salt and pepper
4 lettuce leaves, shredded
4 lemon wedges

Blend the avocado flesh with the mayonnaise. Mix in the crab meat and the green pepper and season to taste with salt and pepper. Put the shredded lettuce into the bottom of four glasses. Heap the avocado mixture on top and serve with lemon wedges.

Quick Liver Pâté

METRIC/IMPERIAL
100 g/4 oz continental liver
  sausage, skinned
50 g/2 oz soft margarine
50 g/2 oz cream cheese
1 tablespoon single cream
squeeze of lemon juice
salt and pepper

AMERICAN
$\frac{1}{4}$ lb continental liver sausage,
  skinned
$\frac{1}{4}$ cup soft margarine
$\frac{1}{4}$ cup cream cheese
1 tablespoon light cream
squeeze of lemon juice
salt and pepper

Cream the liver sausage with the margarine. Beat in the remaining ingredients with salt and pepper to taste. Pack into 4 small pots.

Smoked Mackerel Pâté

METRIC/IMPERIAL
225 g/8 oz smoked mackerel, skinned and boned
50 g/2 oz butter, or 225 g/8 oz cream cheese
1 teaspoon lemon juice
1 garlic clove, crushed
salt
cayenne pepper
melted butter

AMERICAN
½ lb smoked mackerel, skinned and boned
4 tablespoons butter, or 1 cup cream cheese
1 teaspoon lemon juice
1 garlic clove, crushed
salt
cayenne pepper
melted butter

Mash the mackerel flesh with the butter or cream cheese, lemon juice, garlic and salt and cayenne to taste. Pack into small pots and cover with melted butter. Cool.

Variations:
Use kipper fillets, cooked, or any drained canned fish.

Avocado and Mushroom Hors d'oeuvre

METRIC/IMPERIAL
25 g/1 oz butter
2 onions, chopped
4 tablespoons port
2 teaspoons curry powder
2 teaspoons chopped fresh mixed herbs
4 tablespoons chop sauce
1 avocado, peeled, stoned and chopped
225 g/8 oz button mushrooms

AMERICAN
2 tablespoons butter
2 onions, chopped
¼ cup port
2 teaspoons curry powder
2 teaspoons chopped fresh mixed herbs
¼ cup steak sauce
1 avocado, peeled, pitted and chopped
2 cups button mushrooms

Melt the butter in a frying pan (skillet), add the onions and fry until softened. Mix together the port, curry powder, herbs and sauce in a baking dish. Stir in the onions, avocado and mushrooms. Cover and bake in a preheated moderately hot oven (190°C/375°F, Gas Mark 5) for 20 minutes.

AVOCADO AND MUSHROOM STARTER
(Photograph: Corning Limited)

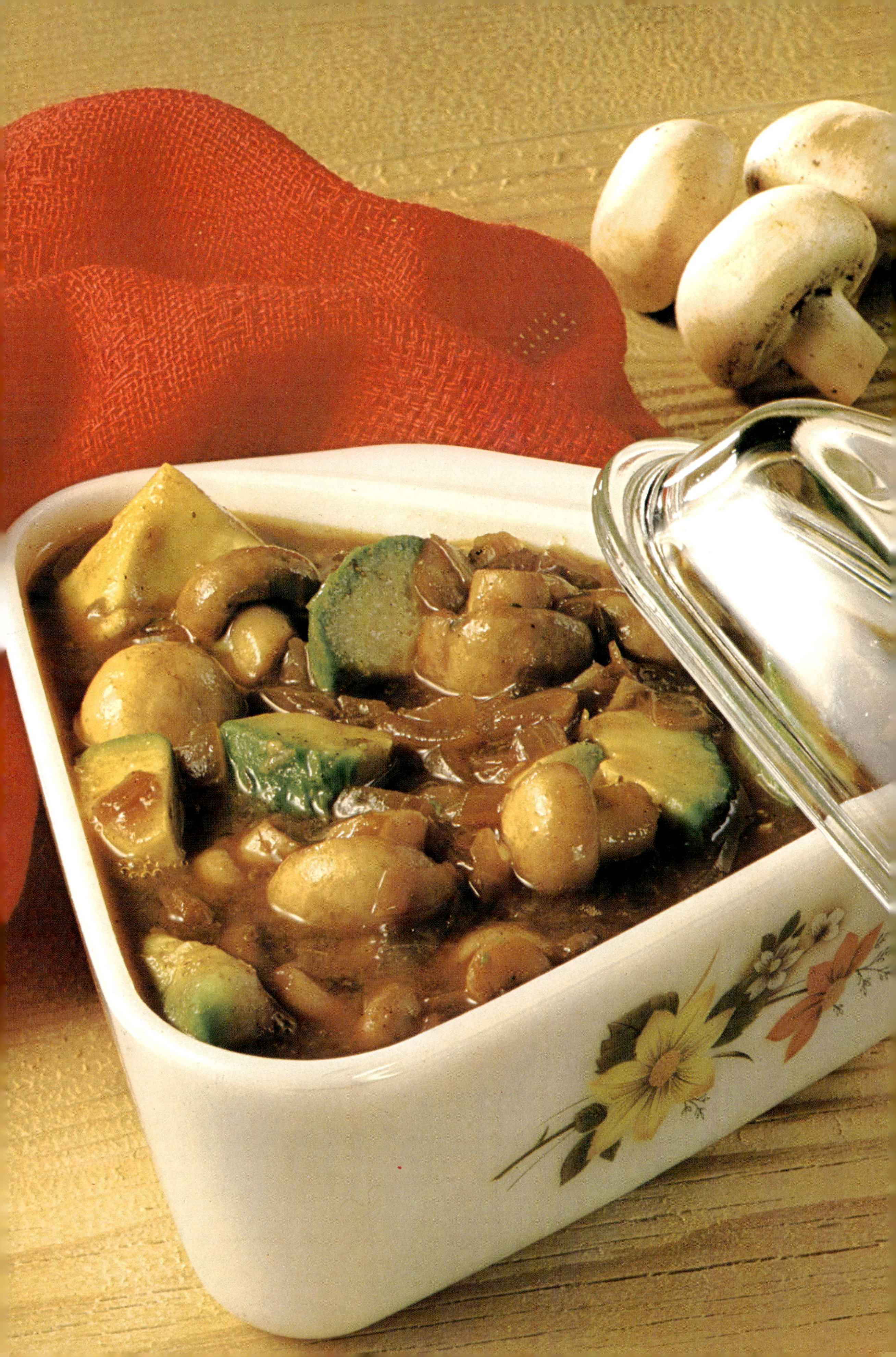

Halibut with Gorgonzola

METRIC/IMPERIAL
4 halibut steaks
225 g/8 oz Gorgonzola or other blue cheese
50 g/2 oz butter
4 tablespoons single cream
salt and pepper

AMERICAN
4 halibut steaks
½ lb Gorgonzola or other blue cheese
4 tablespoons butter
¼ cup light cream
salt and pepper

Place the halibut steaks in a baking dish. Blend together the cheese, butter and cream. Season to taste with salt and pepper. Spread the mixture on the fish and grill (broil) for 10 minutes or until the fish is cooked through.

Fish and Chips

METRIC/IMPERIAL
1 kg/2 lb potatoes, peeled and cut into chips
oil for deep frying
salt
4 × 175 g/6 oz fillets of white fish
flour for coating
lemon wedges
Beer batter:
100 g/4 oz flour
pinch of salt
2 tablespoons oil
150 ml/¼ pint light ale
1 large egg white

AMERICAN
2 lb potatoes, peeled and cut into French fries
oil for deep frying
salt
4 × 6 oz fillets of white fish
flour for coating
lemon wedges
Beer batter:
1 cup flour
pinch of salt
2 tablespoons oil
⅔ cup light beer
1 egg white

First make the batter. Sift the flour and salt into a bowl. Make a well in the centre and pour in the oil and beer. Gradually draw the flour into the liquid, mixing to a smooth batter. Leave to rest for 2 hours.

Dry the potatoes thoroughly with paper towels. Heat the oil in a deep fryer to 190°C/375°F. Deep fry the potatoes, in batches, for 10 minutes or until golden brown. Drain on paper towels, sprinkle with salt and keep warm in the oven.

Beat the egg white until stiff and fold into the batter. Coat the fish lightly with flour, then dip into the batter. Lower the fish into the hot oil and deep fry for 4 to 5 minutes or until crisp and golden brown. Drain on paper towels.

Serve the fish and chips (French fries) piping hot, with lemon wedges.

Fish with Provençal Sauce

METRIC/IMPERIAL
4 white fish steaks
salt and pepper
25 g/1 oz butter
2 tablespoons single cream
100 g/4 oz cheese, grated
Sauce:
15 g/½ oz butter
1 onion, sliced
15 g/½ oz flour
150 ml/¼ pint stock
150 ml/¼ pint tomato purée
2 black olives, stoned and sliced
2 green olives, stoned and sliced
salt and pepper

AMERICAN
4 white fish steaks
salt and pepper
2 tablespoons butter
2 tablespoons light cream
1 cup grated cheese
Sauce:
1 tablespoon butter
1 onion, sliced
2 tablespoons flour
⅔ cup stock
⅔ cup tomato paste
2 ripe olives, pitted and sliced
2 green olives, pitted and sliced
salt and pepper

Season the fish with salt and pepper and place on the grill (broiler) rack. Melt the butter, mix with the cream and brush over the fish. Grill (broil) the fish until it is cooked, turning once.

Meanwhile, make the sauce. Melt the butter in a saucepan, add the onion and fry until softened. Stir in the flour and cook for 2 minutes, then gradually stir in the stock. Bring to the boil, stirring. Add the tomato purée (paste), olives and salt and pepper to taste, mix well and simmer for 5 minutes.

Sprinkle the cheese over the fish and continue cooking until the cheese is melted and golden brown.

Place the fish on a heated serving plate and pour over the sauce.

Marinated Lamb Kebabs

METRIC/IMPERIAL
½ leg of lamb, boned and cut into 2.5 cm/1 inch cubes
Selection of fruit and vegetables, e.g. mushrooms, shallots, tomatoes, pineapple cubes, pieces of green or red pepper, orange segments, celery, etc.

Marinade:
4 tablespoons natural yogurt
juice of ½ lemon
salt and pepper
½ onion, grated

AMERICAN
½ leg of lamb, boned and cut into 1 inch cubes
Selection of fruit and vegetables, e.g. mushrooms, shallots, tomatoes, pineapple cubes, pieces of green or red pepper, orange segments, celery, etc.

Marinade:
¼ cup unflavored yogurt
juice of ½ lemon
salt and pepper
½ onion, grated

Mix the ingredients for the marinade in a bowl, add the meat cubes and leave to marinate for 24 hours.

Drain the meat, reserving the marinade. Thread the meat onto skewers, alternating with the chosen fruit and vegetables. Grill (broil) for 10 to 15 minutes, basting with the marinade and turning frequently. Serve on a bed of savoury rice with a green salad.

Crispy Lamb Fries

METRIC/IMPERIAL
500 g/1 lb minced lamb
100 g/4 oz fresh bread crumbs
1 onion, chopped
3 sticks celery, chopped
½ red pepper, cored, seeded and chopped
½ green pepper, cored, seeded and chopped
grated rind of 1 lemon
2 teaspoons salt
½ teaspoon pepper
2 teaspoons Worcestershire sauce
1 egg, beaten
dry bread crumbs for coating
oil for deep frying

AMERICAN
2 cups ground lamb
2 cups fresh bread crumbs
1 onion, chopped
3 stalks celery, chopped
½ red pepper, cored, seeded and chopped
½ green pepper, cored, seeded and chopped
grated rind of 1 lemon
2 teaspoons salt
½ teaspoon pepper
2 teaspoons Worcestershire sauce
1 egg, beaten
dry bread crumbs for coating
oil for deep frying

Mix together the lamb, fresh bread crumbs, onion, celery, peppers, lemon rind, salt, pepper and Worcestershire sauce. Divide into 8 and form into sausage shapes. Dip into the egg, then coat in dry bread crumbs. Deep fry for 5 to 10 minutes or until golden. Serve with sauce and salad.

CRISPY LAMB FRIES
(Photograph: New Zealand Lamb)

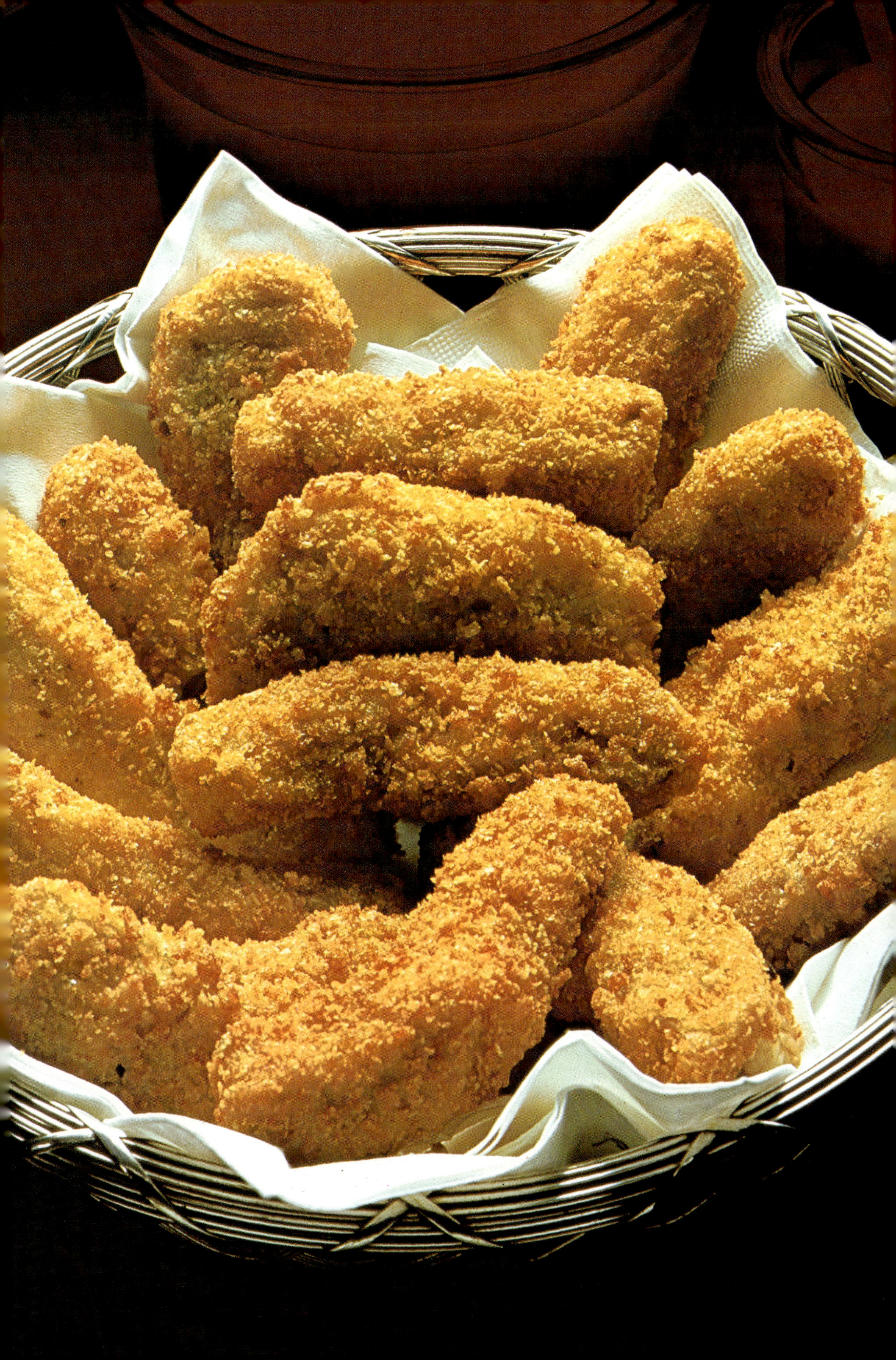

Duckling with Bean Sprouts

METRIC/IMPERIAL
2 tablespoons dripping
100 g/4 oz mushrooms, sliced
4 sticks celery, chopped
4 oz cooked peas or mixed vegetables
500 g/1 lb fresh bean sprouts
the meat from 1 cooked duckling, cut into strips
1 tablespoon soy sauce

AMERICAN
2 tablespoons drippings
1 cup sliced mushrooms
4 stalks celery, chopped
1 cup cooked peas or mixed vegetables
1 lb fresh bean sprouts
the meat from 1 cooked duckling, cut into strips
1 tablespoon soy sauce

Heat the dripping in a large frying pan (skillet), add the mushrooms and fry until tender. Stir in the celery, peas or mixed vegetables, bean sprouts and duckling. Heat through, stirring. Add the soy sauce and serve.

Duckling Sweet and Sour

METRIC/IMPERIAL
4 tablespoons soft brown sugar
2 tablespoons cornflour
2 tablespoons water
4 tablespoons tomato purée
4 tablespoons wine vinegar
2 tablespoons soy sauce
2 tablespoons dry sherry
300 ml/½ pint stock
2 tablespoons dripping
1 green pepper, cored, seeded and chopped
1 carrot, thinly sliced
the meat from 1 cooked duckling, cut into strips
2 oranges, segmented
5 small gherkins, thinly sliced

AMERICAN
¼ cup light brown sugar
2 tablespoons cornstarch
2 tablespoons water
¼ cup tomato paste
¼ cup wine vinegar
2 tablespoons soy sauce
2 tablespoons dry sherry
1¼ cups stock
2 tablespoons drippings
1 green pepper, cored, seeded and chopped
1 carrot, thinly sliced
the meat from 1 cooked duckling, cut into strips
2 oranges, segmented
5 small gherkins, thinly sliced

Mix together the sugar, cornflour (cornstarch), water, tomato purée (paste), vinegar, soy sauce, sherry and stock. Set aside.

Heat the dripping in a frying pan (skillet), add the green pepper and carrot and stir-fry for 2 minutes. Stir in the vinegar mixture and bring to the boil, stirring. Add the meat, orange segments and gherkins and stir-fry for 2 minutes. Serve with freshly boiled rice or noodles.

Devilled Grilled (Broiled) Chicken

METRIC/IMPERIAL
1 chicken
50 g/2 oz butter, melted
salt and pepper
2 tablespoons bread crumbs
Devil sauce:
75 g/3 oz butter
1 teaspoon prepared mustard
½ teaspoon paprika
½ teaspoon salt
cayenne pepper
1 teaspoon vinegar

AMERICAN
1 chicken
4 tablespoons butter, melted
salt and pepper
2 tablespoons bread crumbs
Devil sauce:
6 tablespoons butter
1 teaspoon prepared mustard
½ teaspoon paprika
½ teaspoon salt
cayenne pepper
1 teaspoon vinegar

Split the chicken through the backbone. Flatten out well. Turn the wings back and skewer them into position. Brush with the melted butter and season well with salt and pepper. Grill (broil), first the skin side and then the other, brushing with more butter.

To make the sauce, cream the butter with the mustard and mix in the paprika, salt, cayenne and vinegar. Brush the sauce over the chicken. Sprinkle with the bread crumbs and grill (broil) until golden.

Skewered Sausages

METRIC/IMPERIAL
500 g/1 lb sausages
1 × 500 g/1 lb 3 oz can new potatoes, drained
225 g/8 oz tomatoes, halved
2 tablespoons thick marmalade
150 ml/¼ pint stock
1 teaspoon tomato purée
1 teaspoon Worcestershire sauce
1 tablespoon cornflour
1 tablespoon water

AMERICAN
1 lb sausages
1 × 1 lb 3 oz can new potatoes, drained
½ lb tomatoes, halved
2 tablespoons thick marmalade
⅔ cup stock
1 teaspoon tomato paste
1 teaspoon Worcestershire sauce
1 tablespoon cornstarch
1 tablespoon water

Thread the sausages, potatoes and tomatoes on 4 skewers. Put the marmalade, stock, tomato purée (paste) and Worcestershire sauce in a saucepan, bring to the boil and simmer for 5 minutes. Dissolve the cornflour (cornstarch) in the water. Add to the pan and return to the boil, stirring until the sauce thickens. Brush the sausages and vegetables with the sauce and cook under the grill (broiler), turning and basting with the sauce frequently. Serve with savoury rice and salad.

St David's Crispy Bake

METRIC/IMPERIAL
500 g/1 lb leeks, washed and sliced
350 g/12 oz cooking apples, sliced
water for cooking
8 slices of cooked ham
1 packet white sauce mix
milk
½ teaspoon mustard powder
1 small bag cheese and onion crisps

AMERICAN
4 cups washed and sliced leeks
3 cups sliced baking apples
water for cooking
8 slices of cooked ham
1 package white sauce mix
milk
½ teaspoon mustard powder
½ cup cheese and onion chips

Cook the leeks and apples in a very small amount of water; drain well. Place a portion of the mixture on each slice of ham and roll up. Arrange them in a greased ovenproof dish. Make up the white sauce according to the instructions, add the mustard powder and pour over the ham rolls. Crush the crisps (chips) and sprinkle over the top. Bake in a moderately hot oven (190°C/375°F, Gas Mark 5) for 15 minutes.

Onion and Mushroom Steaklets

METRIC/IMPERIAL
25 g/1 oz butter
4 tablespoons oil
2 onions, finely chopped
225 g/8 oz mushrooms, chopped
½ teaspoon sage
1 clove garlic, crushed
750 g/1½ lb minced beef
salt and pepper

AMERICAN
2 tablespoons butter
4 tablespoons oil
2 onions, finely chopped
2 cups chopped mushrooms
½ teaspoon sage
1 clove garlic, crushed
3 cups ground beef
salt and pepper

Heat the butter and 2 tablespoons of the oil. Gently fry the onion and mushrooms for about 4 minutes. Mix in the sage and garlic and cook for 1 minute. Allow to cool. Mix the onion and mushrooms into the beef and season with salt and pepper. Divide the mixture into 8 flat round patties. Fry slowly in the remaining oil for about 6 minutes on each side.

ST DAVID'S CRISPY BAKE
(Photograph: Milk Marketing Board)

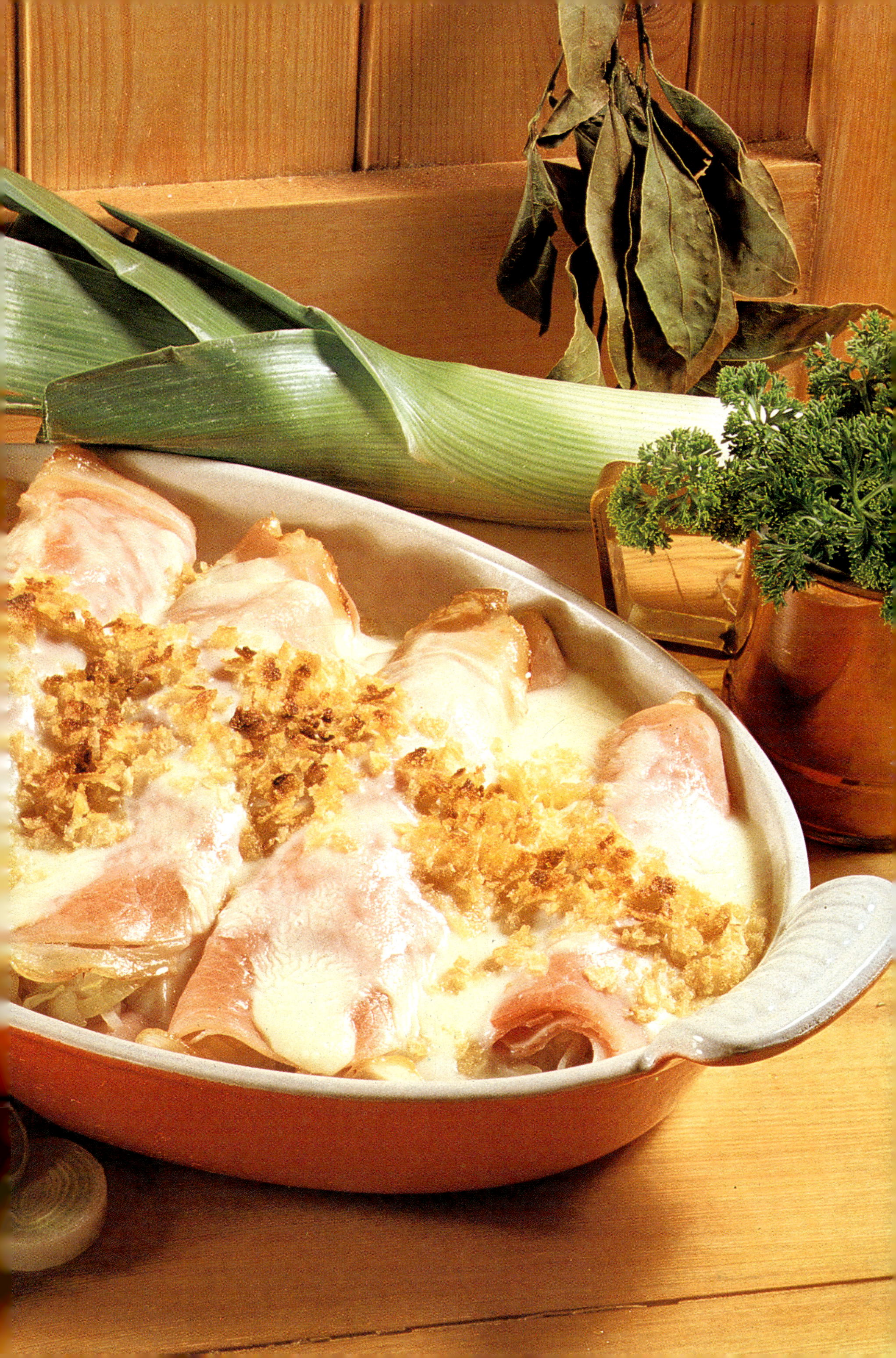

Oeufs à la Valenciana

METRIC/IMPERIAL
2 tablespoons oil
225 g/8 oz long grain rice
900 ml/2½ pints boiling water
salt
75 g/3 oz butter
2 onions, sliced
1 garlic clove, crushed
4 tomatoes, skinned
4 tablespoons chopped pimiento
50 g/2 oz almonds, chopped
50 g/2 oz raisins
2 bananas, sliced
8 eggs
Garnish:
tomato wedges
parsley

AMERICAN
2 tablespoons oil
2 cups long grain rice
4 cups boiling water
salt
6 tablespoons butter
2 onions, sliced
1 garlic clove, crushed
4 tomatoes, skinned
¼ cup chopped pimiento
½ cup chopped almonds
⅓ cup raisins
2 bananas, sliced
8 eggs
Garnish:
tomato wedges
parsley

Heat the oil in a saucepan, add the rice and fry until it looks transparent. Pour on the boiling water, add salt and cook for about 12 minutes.

Meanwhile, melt 25 g/1 oz (2 tablespoons) of the butter in a frying pan (skillet), add the onions, garlic and tomatoes and fry until the onions are softened. Stir in the pimiento, almonds, raisins and bananas and heat through gently. Drain the rice, if necessary, and stir into the frying pan (skillet). Keep hot.

Melt the remaining butter in another frying pan (skillet), add the eggs in batches, and fry until set. Pile the rice mixture on a heated serving platter and arrange the eggs on top. Garnish with tomato wedges and parsley.

SHORT AND SWEET

Malvern Pudding

METRIC/IMPERIAL
1 teaspoon ground cinnamon
1 teaspoon ground mixed spice
500 g/1 lb sweetened apple purée
300 ml/½ pint canned custard
25 g/1 oz cornflakes, crushed
2 tablespoons chopped nuts

AMERICAN
1 teaspoon ground cinnamon
1 teaspoon apple pie spice
2 cups sweetened apple purée
1¼ cups canned custard sauce
1 cup cornflakes, crushed
2 tablespoons chopped nuts

Mix the spices into the apple purée. Divide between 4 flameproof dishes. Pour the custard over the apple. Mix the cornflakes with the nuts. Sprinkle over the top. Grill (broil) until golden.

Strawberries Cordon Bleu

METRIC/IMPERIAL
500 g/1 lb strawberries
100 g/4 oz ratafias or macaroons, crushed
grated rind and juice of 1 orange
25 g/1 oz caster sugar
150 ml/¼ pint double cream
4 shortbread fingers

AMERICAN
1 lb strawberries
1 cup crushed ratafias or macaroons
grated rind and juice of 1 orange
2 tablespoons sugar
⅔ cup heavy cream
4 shortbread fingers

Mix the strawberries with the ratafia or macaroon crumbs and orange rind. Divide into 4 glasses. Add the sugar to the orange juice and stir to dissolve. Whip the cream until thick and fold in the orange juice. Pile the cream on the strawberries. Chill, then serve with the shortbread fingers.

Tangy Pineapple Meringue

METRIC/IMPERIAL
3 trifle sponge cakes
3 tablespoons sherry
1 tablespoon lemon juice
1 × 425 g/15 oz can pineapple rings
2 egg whites
100 g/4 oz caster sugar
Sauce:
1 teaspoon arrowroot
1 teaspoon sugar
1 teaspoon lemon juice
juice from the canned pineapple

AMERICAN
3 slices of pound cake
3 tablespoons sherry
1 tablespoon lemon juice
1 × 15 oz can pineapple rings
2 egg whites
½ cup sugar
Sauce:
1 teaspoon arrowroot flour
1 teaspoon sugar
1 teaspoon lemon juice
juice from the canned pineapple

Cut the cakes in half lengthways and place in the bottom of a shallow ovenproof dish. Pour over the sherry and lemon juice. Drain the pineapple rings, reserving the juice. Place the pineapple rings on the cake.

Beat the egg whites until stiff. Add 2 tablespoons of the sugar and continue beating for 1 minute. Fold in the remaining sugar. Spoon or pipe onto the pineapple. Bake in a preheated moderately hot oven (190°C/375°F, Gas Mark 5) for 8 to 10 minutes.

Meanwhile, dissolve the arrowroot in the reserved pineapple juice in a saucepan. Add the sugar and lemon juice and bring to the boil, stirring. Simmer until thickened. Serve with the pudding.

Crispy Pineapple Sundae

METRIC/IMPERIAL
50 g/2 oz butter
75 g/3 oz ginger nut biscuits, crushed
50 g/2 oz cornflakes, crushed
25 g/1 oz walnuts, chopped
1 × 350 g/12 oz can pineapple chunks, drained
1 tablespoon ginger marmalade
300 ml/½ pint canned custard
whipped cream to decorate

AMERICAN
4 tablespoons butter
¾ cup crushed ginger snap cookies
2 cups cornflakes, crushed
¼ cup chopped walnuts
1 × 12 oz can pineapple chunks, drained
1 tablespoon ginger marmalade
1¼ cups canned custard sauce
whipped cream to decorate

Melt the butter in a saucepan and mix in the biscuit (cookie) crumbs, cornflakes and nuts. Cool. Add the pineapple and marmalade to the custard and mix well. Divide the custard and crumb mixture between 4 glasses to form layers, finishing with custard. Decorate with whipped cream and serve chilled.

CRISPY PINEAPPLE SUNDAE
(Photograph: Milk Marketing Board)

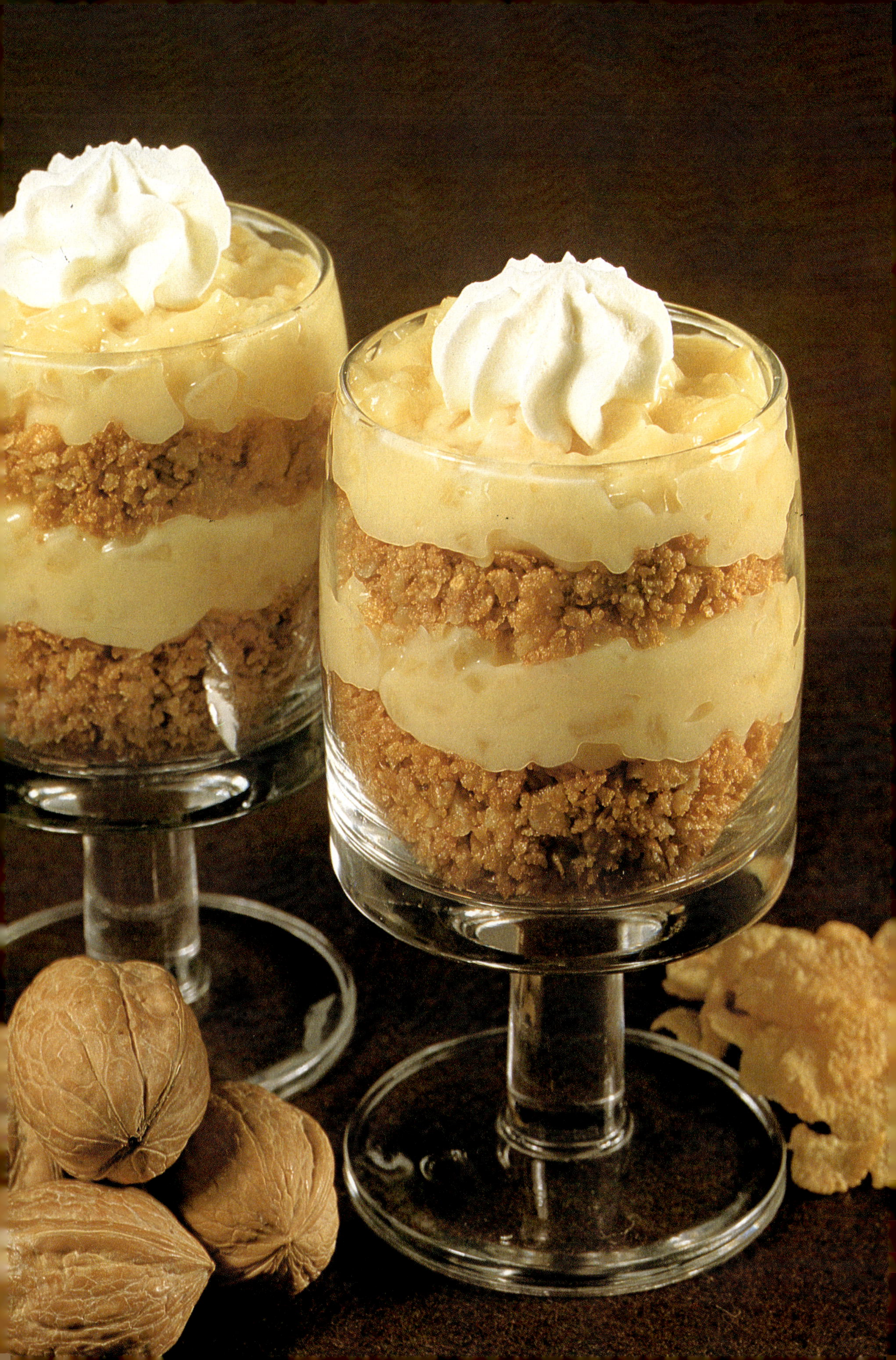

Lemon Dreams

METRIC/IMPERIAL
4 tablespoons lemon squash
100 g/4 oz caster sugar
25 g/1 oz cornflour
40 g/1½ oz butter
150 ml/¼ pint milk
2 eggs, separated
150 ml/¼ pint natural yogurt
angelica to decorate

AMERICAN
¼ cup sweetened lemon drink concentrate
½ cup sugar
¼ cup cornstarch
3 tablespoons butter
⅔ cup milk
2 eggs, separated
⅔ cup unflavored yogurt
angelica to decorate

Place the squash (drink), sugar, cornflour (cornstarch), butter and milk in a saucepan. Bring to the boil, stirring. Remove from the heat and add the egg yolks. Beat the egg whites until stiff and fold in the lemon mixture and yogurt. Divide between 4 glasses and decorate with angelica. Chill for 20 minutes.

Lemon Cream Cheese

METRIC/IMPERIAL
175 g/6 oz cream cheese
50 g/2 oz caster sugar
grated rind and juice of ½ lemon
2 eggs, separated
150 ml/¼ pint double cream
To decorate:
chopped nuts
grated chocolate

AMERICAN
¾ cup cream cheese
¼ cup sugar
grated rind and juice of ½ lemon
2 eggs, separated
⅔ cup heavy cream
To decorate:
chopped nuts
grated chocolate

Cream together the cheese, sugar, lemon rind and juice and egg yolks. Whip the cream until thick, and beat the egg whites until stiff. Fold the cream and egg whites into the cheese mixture. Serve in glasses, decorated with nuts and chocolate.

Variations:
The cheese mixture may be used as a filling for a baked pastry case or crushed biscuit (graham cracker) crust.

Cheese Cream with Fruit Purée

METRIC/IMPERIAL
225 g/8 oz cream cheese
50 g/2 oz caster sugar
2 tablespoons single cream
1 egg yolk
2 drops of vanilla essence
1 teaspoon lemon juice
2 tablespoons blackcurrant purée
blackcurrants to decorate
sponge fingers

AMERICAN
1 cup cream cheese
¼ cup sugar
2 tablespoons light cream
1 egg yolk
2 drops of vanilla extract
1 teaspoon lemon juice
2 tablespoons blackberry purée
blackberries to decorate
lady fingers

Blend together all the ingredients except the fruit purée. Divide the purée between 4 glasses. Pour in the cream cheese mixture. Chill. Decorate with blackcurrants (blackberries), and serve with sponge fingers (lady fingers).

Toffee Meringue Glacé

METRIC/IMPERIAL
4 scoops vanilla ice cream
4 meringue shells
Sauce:
4 tablespoons brown sugar
1 tablespoon golden syrup
2 tablespoons milk
25 g/1 oz butter
2 drops of vanilla essence

AMERICAN
4 scoops vanilla ice cream
4 meringue shells
Sauce:
¼ cup brown sugar
1 tablespoon golden or light corn syrup
2 tablespoons milk
2 tablespoons butter
2 drops of vanilla extract

Place all the sauce ingredients in a saucepan and bring slowly to the boil, stirring to dissolve the sugar. Boil for 3 to 4 minutes.

Place the scoops of ice cream in the meringue shells. Pour a little sauce over the ice cream. Serve the rest of the sauce separately.

Black Cherry Waffles

METRIC/IMPERIAL
8 frozen waffles
150 ml/¼ pint double cream
2 tablespoons cassis
1 × 425 g/15 oz can stoned black cherries, drained

AMERICAN
8 frozen waffles
⅔ cup heavy cream
2 tablespoons cassis
1 × 15 oz can pitted black cherries, drained

Bake or toast the waffles according to the directions on the packet. Lightly whip the cream and cassis together. Spoon the mixture over the hot waffles and top with the cherries.

Variations:
Top hot waffles with sliced bananas and chocolate sauce; or canned pear halves, chocolate sauce and chopped pistachio nuts; or sliced strawberries and whipped cream.

Apricot Popovers

METRIC/IMPERIAL
1 × 450 g/1 lb can apricot halves, drained
50 g/2 oz butter
Batter:
50 g/2 oz flour
pinch of salt
1 egg
150 ml/¼ pint milk

AMERICAN
1 × 1 lb can apricot halves, drained
4 tablespoons butter
Batter:
½ cup flour
pinch of salt
1 egg
⅔ cup milk

Place an apricot half in each of 12 deep patty tins and add a smear of butter to each. Bake in a preheated hot oven (220°C/425°F, Gas Mark 7) for 3 minutes.

Meanwhile make the batter: sift the flour and salt into a bowl. Beat in the egg and half the milk. Stir in the remaining milk. Spoon 1 tablespoon of batter over each apricot and return to the oven. Bake for about 20 minutes or until well risen and crisp. Serve immediately.
Makes 12

BLACK CHERRY WAFFLES
(Photograph: Kellogg Company)

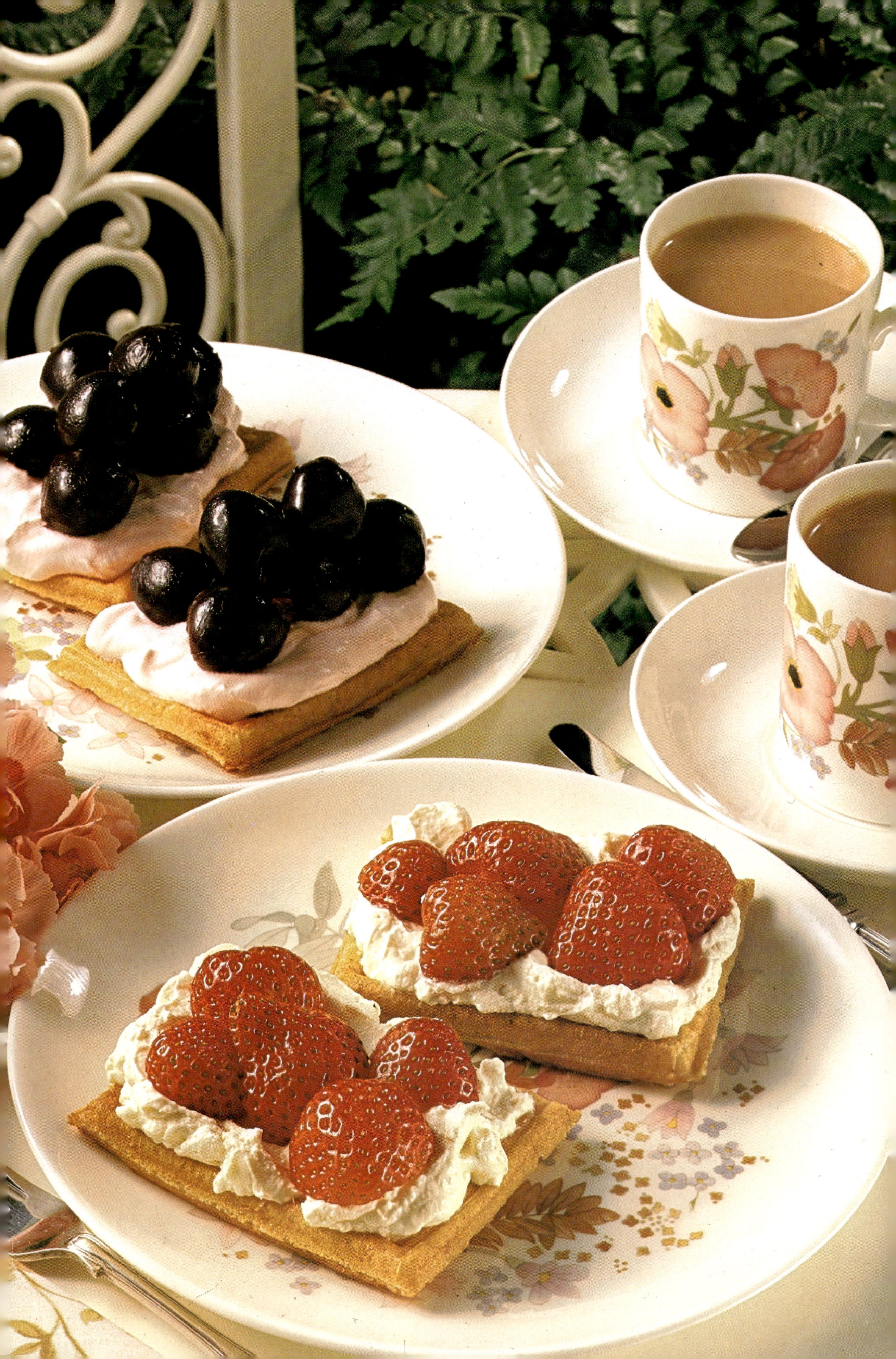

Rhubarb Compôte

METRIC/IMPERIAL
1 × 500 g/1 lb 3 oz can rhubarb
75 g/3 oz sultanas
50 g/2 oz demerara sugar
1 banana, sliced
pinch of ground cinnamon

AMERICAN
1 × 1 lb 3 oz can rhubarb
½ cup seedless white raisins
⅓ cup raw brown sugar
1 banana, sliced
pinch of ground cinnamon

Heat the ingredients in a saucepan. Serve immediately.

Whisky and Oatmeal Syllabub

METRIC/IMPERIAL
25 g/1 oz medium oatmeal
300 ml/½ pint double cream
100 g/4 oz golden syrup
5 tablespoons whisky
1 teaspoon lemon juice

AMERICAN
¼ cup oatmeal
1¼ cups heavy cream
⅓ cup golden or light corn syrup
5 tablespoons whisky
1 teaspoon lemon juice

Toast the oatmeal until golden brown. Whip the cream until thick. Mix together the syrup, whisky and lemon juice. Fold into the cream with most of the oatmeal. Pile into glasses and chill. Sprinkle with the remaining oatmeal.

Gooseberry Fluff

METRIC/IMPERIAL
300 ml/½ pint milk
25 g/1 oz semolina

2 eggs, separated
50 g/2 oz caster sugar
300 ml/½ pint thick gooseberry purée
1 tablespoon lemon juice
grated chocolate to decorate

AMERICAN
1¼ cups milk
3 tablespoons semolina flour or cream of wheat
2 eggs, separated
¼ cup sugar
1¼ cups thick gooseberry purée
1 tablespoon lemon juice
grated chocolate to decorate

Heat the milk in a saucepan, add the semolina and cook, stirring, for 5 minutes or until thickened. Remove from the heat. Add the egg yolks and sugar, then fold in the gooseberry purée and lemon juice. Beat the egg whites until stiff and fold into the fruit mixture. Spoon into glasses and chill. Decorate with grated chocolate.

Creole Bake

METRIC/IMPERIAL
4 bananas
1 tablespoon cornflour
2 tablespoons cocoa powder
150 ml/¼ pint milk
25 g/1 oz demerara sugar
2 teaspoons rum
150 ml/¼ pint double cream, whipped

AMERICAN
4 bananas
1 tablespoon cornstarch
2 tablespoons cocoa powder
⅔ cup milk
2 tablespoons raw brown sugar
2 teaspoons rum
⅔ cup heavy cream, whipped

Bake the bananas in their skins in a preheated moderately hot oven (200°C/400°F, Gas Mark 6) for 15 minutes or until the skins turn black. Dissolve the cornflour (cornstarch) and cocoa in a little of the milk. Add to the remaining milk and the sugar in a saucepan. Bring to the boil, stirring. Stir in the rum off the heat.

Peel the bananas and arrange in a warm dish. Pipe the cream around the bananas. Pour over the sauce.

Custard and Apple Coupe

METRIC/IMPERIAL
1 × 383 g/13½ oz can apple slices
2 tablespoons orange squash, undiluted
1 tablespoon caster sugar
1 × 425 g/15 oz can custard
1 × 200 g/7 oz can cream
1 tablespoon redcurrant jelly

AMERICAN
1 × 13½ oz can apple slices
2 tablespoons sweetened orange drink concentrate
1 tablespoon sugar
1 × 15 oz can custard sauce
1 × 7 oz can cream
1 tablespoon redcurrant jelly

Mix the apple slices with the orange drink and sugar. Fill individual glasses with layers of apple slices and custard. Top with the cream and decorate with redcurrant jelly.

Luxury Coffee Sundae

METRIC/IMPERIAL
8 scoops of coffee ice cream
4 pieces stem ginger, chopped
8 tablespoons ginger syrup
4 tablespoons whipped cream
100 g/4 oz plain chocolate, grated
4 maraschino cherries

AMERICAN
8 scoops of coffee ice cream
4 pieces preserved ginger, chopped
½ cup ginger syrup
¼ cup whipped cream
4 squares dark chocolate, grated
4 maraschino cherries

Put 2 scoops of ice cream in each sundae dish. Top with the ginger, ginger syrup and cream. Sprinkle with grated chocolate and top with a cherry.

CUSTARD AND APPLE COUPE
(Photograph: Canned Food Advisory Service)

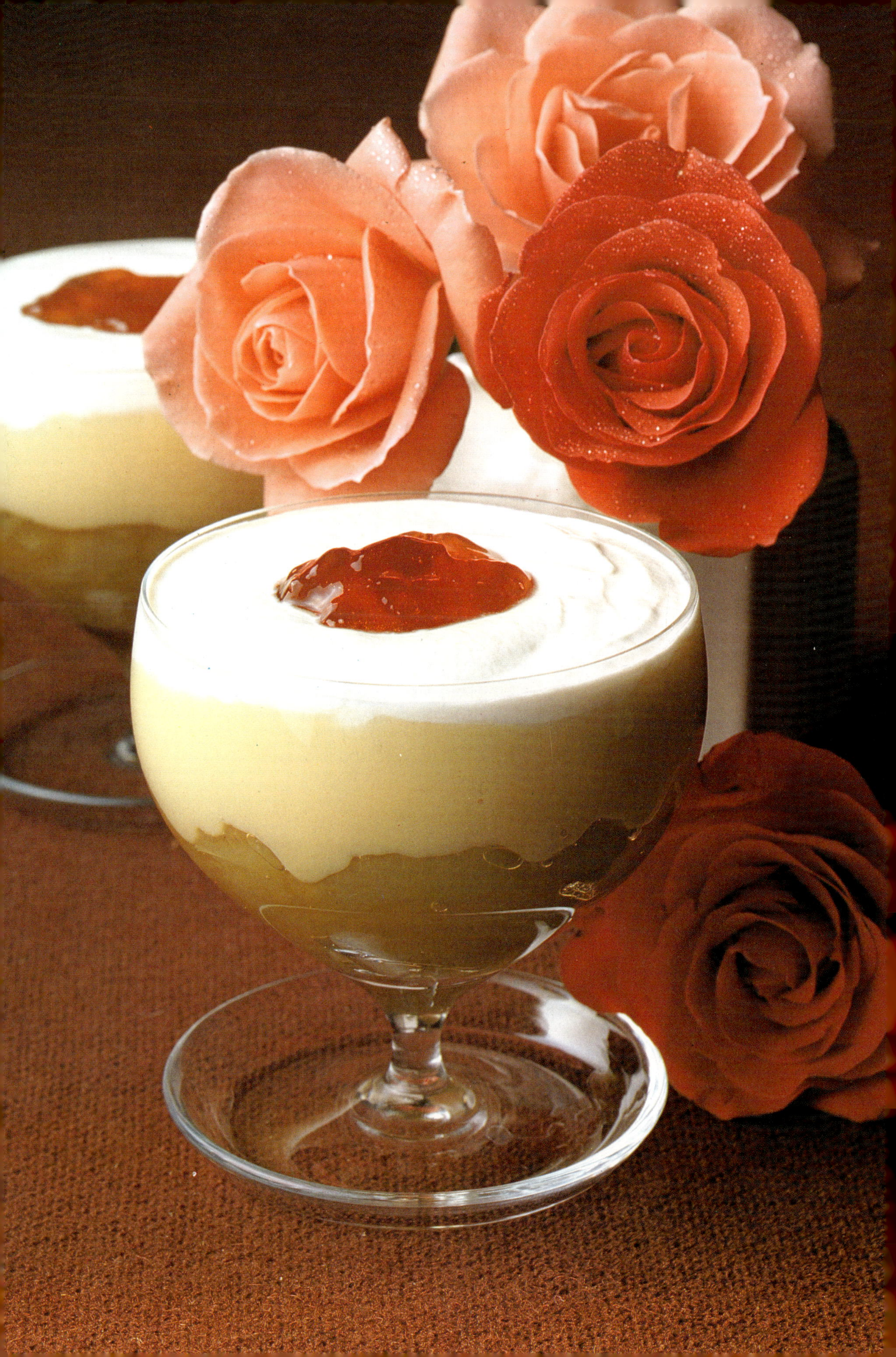

Sweet Banana Crêpes

METRIC/IMPERIAL
100 g/4 oz flour
1 egg and 1 yolk
300 ml/½ pint milk
1 teaspoon lemon juice
1 tablespoon oil
oil for cooking
Filling:
6 bananas, sliced
2 tablespoons lemon juice
300 ml/½ pint double cream, whipped
50 g/2 oz walnuts, chopped
Topping:
½ banana, sliced
chocolate sauce
chopped walnuts

AMERICAN
1 cup flour
1 egg and 1 yolk
1¼ cups milk
1 teaspoon lemon juice
1 tablespoon oil
oil for cooking
Filling:
6 bananas, sliced
2 tablespoons lemon juice
1¼ cups heavy cream, whipped
½ cup chopped walnuts
Topping:
½ banana, sliced
chocolate sauce
chopped walnuts

Sift the flour into a mixing bowl. Make a well in the centre and add the egg and egg yolk. Gradually stir in the flour with the milk. Add the lemon juice and oil and beat to make a smooth batter. Leave to rest for 10 minutes. Use the batter to make 8 small crêpes (see page 22 for method). Keep warm.

For the filling, toss the banana slices in the lemon juice to prevent discoloration. Stir in the cream and walnuts. Divide between the crêpes and roll them up. Top with banana slices, chocolate sauce and nuts.

Alternative fillings:
Apple
Mix 300 ml/½ pint (1¼ cups) sweetened apple purée with 50 g/2 oz sultanas (⅓ cup seedless white raisins), and a pinch of ground cinnamon. Dredge with icing (confectioners') sugar.

Chestnut
Use 1 × 225 g/8 oz can sweetened chestnut purée.

Chocolate and Cream
Fold 50 g/2 oz plain (dark) chocolate, melted and cooled, into 300 ml/½ pint (1¼ cups) whipped cream with 25 g/1 oz (¼ cup) nuts, chopped.

Royal
Mix 1 × 425 g/15 oz can apricot halves, drained, with 100 g/4 oz mixed black (purple) and green (white) grapes, halved and seeded, 1 tablespoon honey, 1 tablespoon lime juice and 25 g/1 oz (¼ cup) toasted hazelnuts, chopped.

Christmas Alaska

METRIC/IMPERIAL
4–6 slices Christmas pudding or cake
2 tablespoons brandy or sherry
4–6 scoops ice cream
150 ml/¼ pint double cream, whipped
3 egg whites
175 g/6 oz castor sugar
To decorate:
glacé cherries
angelica

AMERICAN
4–6 slices plum pudding or rich fruit cake
2 tablespoons brandy or sherry
4–6 scoops ice cream
⅔ cup heavy cream, whipped
3 egg whites
¾ cup sugar
To decorate:
candied cherries
angelica

Arrange the pudding or cake slices on an ovenproof plate. Soak with the brandy or sherry. Pile the ice cream on top and cover with the cream.

Beat the egg whites until stiff. Add 3 tablespoons of the sugar and continue beating for 1 minute. Fold in the remaining sugar. Completely cover the ice cream and cream with the meringue. Bake in a preheated moderately hot oven (200°C/400°F, Gas Mark 6) for about 3 minutes or until the meringue is just tinted golden. Decorate with cherries and angelica. Serve immediately.

Little Jiffy Dishy

METRIC/IMPERIAL
4 medium cooking apples, peeled, cored and chopped
100 g/4 oz sugar
1 tablespoon flour
1 tablespoon lemon juice
1 teaspoon ground cinnamon
50 g/2 oz butter
2 tablespoons water
100 g/4 oz digestive biscuits, crushed
whipped cream

AMERICAN
4 medium baking apples, peeled, cored and chopped
½ cup sugar
1 tablespoon flour
1 tablespoon lemon juice
1 teaspoon ground cinnamon
4 tablespoons butter
2 tablespoons water
1 cup crushed graham crackers
whipped cream

Combine all the ingredients except the crushed biscuits (crackers) and cream in a saucepan. Cook, stirring occasionally, until the apples are tender. Put the biscuit (cracker) crumbs into glasses. Pile on the apple mixture. Cool. Serve with whipped cream.

INDEX

Alaska, Christmas 75
Apples:
    Apple crêpes 74
    Custard and apple coupe 72
    Little jiffy dishy 75
    Malvern pudding 63
Apricot popovers 68
Aubergine rarebit 12
Avocado and mushroom hors d'oeuvre 52
Avocado cocktail 51

Bacon:
    Corn and bacon rolls 35
    Leek and bacon crêpes 22
    Toasted bacon and mushroom sandwich 39
    Tomato crêpes 22
Banana crêpes, sweet 74
Barbecue butter beans 28
Barbecued pork with pineapple 26
Beans:
    Barbecued butter (baby lima) beans 28
    Duckling with bean sprouts 58
    Mixed bean salad 47
    Quick chilli con carne 26
Beef:
    Cheesy beef pizzas 8
    Corned beef crêpes 22
    Fried silverside (corned beef) sandwiches 32
    Moussaka 30
    Onion and mushroom steaklets 60
    Panhandle corned beef hash 28
    Quick chilli con carne 26
    Speedy beef 'n' rice 31
    Tacos 23
Biscuit pizza 11
Black cherry waffles 68
Bratwurst kedgeree 19
Burgers:
    Chilli burgers 24
    Lamburgers 24

Celery:
    Egg and celery loaf 39
Cheese:
    Aubergine rarebit 12

Cheese cream with fruit purée 67
Cheese double deckers 40
Cheesy beef pizzas 8
Cottage toasties 12
Halibut with Gorgonzola 54
Hot cheese soup 50
King Camembert salad 47
Lemon cream cheese 66
Melon and pineapple dip 50
Cherries:
    Black cherry waffles 68
Chestnut crêpes 74
Chicken:
    Chicken and chestnut soup 48
    Chicken and mushrooms in potato nests 27
    Chicken crêpes 22
    Chinese noodles 20
    Devilled grilled (broiled) chicken 59
    Devilled potato and chicken salad 43
    Russian salad 44
Chilli burgers 24
Chilli con carne, Quick 26
Chinese noodles 20
Chips 54
Chocolate and cream crêpes 74
Chowder, salmon 23
Christmas Alaska 75
Club sandwich 38
Continental salad 43
Corn:
    Corn and bacon fritters 31
    Corn and bacon rolls 35
    Corn scramble 16
    Salmon chowder 23
Corned beef *see under* Beef
Cottage toasties 12
Crab:
    Avocado cocktail 51
    Crab and tomato toasts 34
Creole bake 71
Crêpes, savoury 22
Crêpes, sweet 74
Crispy duck salad 46
Crispy lamb fries 56
Crispy pineapple sundae 64

Custard and apple coupe 72
Danish open sandwiches 40
Desserts 63–75
Devilled grilled chicken 59
Devilled potato and chicken salad 43
Devilled sausage toppers 35
Dip, melon and pineapple 50
Duck:
    Crispy duck salad 46
    Duckling sweet and sour 58
    Duckling with bean sprouts 58

Eggplant rarebit 12
Eggs:
    Corn scramble 16
    Egg and celery loaf 39
    Egg and mushroom rarebit 38
    Egg hubble bubble 15
    Eggs Florentine 14
    Kedgeree 19
    Oeufs à la Valenciana 62
    Scrambled eggs supreme 15
    Toasted bacon and mushroom sandwiches 39

Fish and chips 54
Fish with Provençal sauce 55
French dressing 42
Fried silverside sandwiches 32
Fritters, corn and bacon 31

German breakfast platter 18
Gooseberry fluff 71

Haddock:
    Kedgeree 19
    Halibut with Gorgonzola 54
Ham:
    St. David's crispy bake 60
Hors d'oeuvre, avocado and mushroom 52
Hot cheese soup 50

Isle of Skye soup 48

Jubilee toasts 36

Kebab, Pitta 16
Kebabs, Marinated lamb 56
Kedgeree 19
King Camembert salad 47

Lamb:
    Crispy lamb fries 56
    Lamburgers 24
    Marinated lamb kebabs 56
    Pitta kebab 16
Leeks:
    Leek and bacon crêpes 22
    St. David's crispy bake 60
Lemon cream cheese 66
Lemon dreams 66
Little jiffy dishy 75
Liver:
    Quick liver pâté 51
    Thirty-minute pan fry 18
Luxury coffee sundae 72

Malvern pudding 63
Marinated lamb kebabs 56
Mayonnaise 42
Melon and pineapple dip 50
Minced beef:
    Cheesy beef pizzas 8
    Onion and mushroom steaklets 60
    Quick chilli con carne 26
    Speedy beef 'n' rice 31
    Tacos 23
Minced lamb:
    Lamburgers 24
    Crispy lamb fries 56
Mixed bean salad 47
Moussaka 30
Mushrooms:
    Avocado and mushroom hors d'oeuvre 52
    Chicken and mushroom in potato nests 27
    Cottage toasties 12
    Egg and mushroom rarebit 38
    Isle of Skye soup 48
    Onion and mushroom steaklets 60
    Regal toasts 36
    Slimmer's delight 47
    Toasted bacon and mushroom sandwich 39

Noodles, Chinese 20
Noodles Romanoff 20

Oeufs à la Valenciana 62
Onion and mushroom steaklets 60
Open sandwiches, Danish 40

Pancakes *see* Crêpes
Panhandle corned beef hash 28
Pâté, quick liver 51
Pâté, smoked mackerel 52
Pineapple:
    Barbecued pork with pineapple 26
    Crispy pineapple slices 64
    Melon and pineapple dip 50
    Tangy pineapple meringue 64
Pitta kebab 16
Pizzas:
    Cheesy beef pizzas 8
    Potato pizza 27
    Scone (biscuit) pizza 11
Pork with pineapple, barbecued 26
Potatoes:
    Chicken and mushrooms in potato nests 27
    Devilled potato and chicken salad 43
    Fish and chips 54
    Panhandle corned beef hash 28
    Potato pizza 27
    Stuffed baked potatoes 10

Quick chilli con carne 26
Quick liver pâté 51

Rarebit, aubergine 12
Rarebit, egg and mushroom 38
Regal toasts 36
Rhubarb compôte 70
Rice:
    Kedgeree 19
    Speedy beef 'n' rice 31
Royal crêpes 74
Russian salad 44

St David's crispy bake 60
Salad Niçoise 44
Salads, speedy 42–7

Salmon chowder 23
Sandwiches hot and cold 32–41
Sardine toasties 34
Sausages:
    Devilled sausage toppers 35
    Skewered sausages 59
Savoury crêpes 22
Scone pizza 11
Scrambled eggs supreme 15
Silverside sandwiches, fried 32
Skewered sausages 59
Slimmer's delight 47
Smoked mackerel pâté 52
Soups:
    Chicken and chestnut soup 48
    Hot cheese soup 50
    Isle of Skye soup 48
    Speedy beef 'n' rice 31
Spinach:
    Eggs Florentine 14
Steak *see* Beef
Steaklets, onion and mushroom 60
Strawberries Cordon Bleu 63
Stuffed baked potatoes 10
Sundae, luxury coffee 72
Sweet banana crêpes 74
Sweetcorn *see* Corn
Sweets 63–75
Syllabub, whisky and oatmeal 70

Tacos 23
Tangy pineapple meringue 64
Thirty-minute pan fry 18
Toasted bacon and mushroom sandwich 39
Toffee meringue glacé 67
Tomatoes:
    Cottage toasties 12
    Eggs Florentine 14
    Tomato crêpes 22
Toreador crêpes 22
Tuna fish:
    Salad Niçoise 44

Waffles, black cherry 68
Waldorf salad 46
Whisky and oatmeal syllabub 70

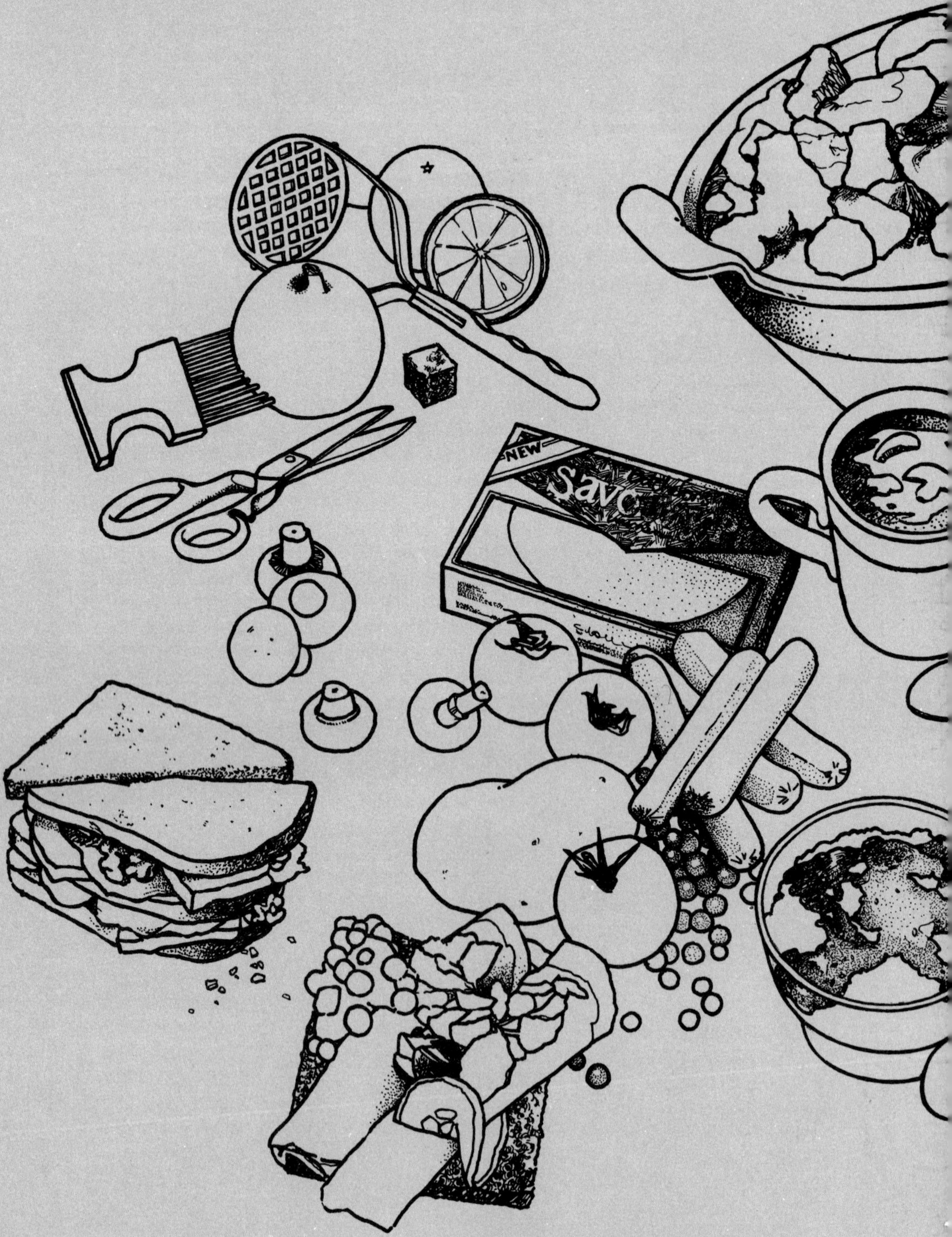
NEW